EDITH WHARTON

1862–1937

Edith Wharton
(about 1884)

Edith Wharton

1862-1937

by OLIVIA COOLIDGE

NEW YORK

CHARLES SCRIBNER'S SONS

ACKNOWLEDGMENTS

The author wishes to thank Messrs. Wayne Andrews, Louis Auchincloss, Donald C. Gallup, Frederick King, William Tyler, and Charles Scribner's Sons for their cooperation and help in her research.

The author gratefully acknowledges permission to quote from letters of Edith Wharton to Mary Cadwalader Jones in the Edith Wharton Collection at Yale University Library.

Grateful acknowledgment is also made to A. Watkins, Inc. for permission to quote from *The Mother's Recompense* by Edith Wharton and to Charles Scribner's Sons for permission to quote from other works of Edith Wharton.

CONTENTS

INTRODUCTION

THE life of Edith Wharton is the story of a strong creative instinct. Neither Edith's parents nor her brothers
made any mark in the world, and her husband had no
profession. She felt no economic pressure to write, while
every influence throughout her formative years was
dead against it. Yet Edith was possessed of a driving
force sufficient to overcome her own undisciplined habits, the distractions of a wealthy life, and the indifference
of everyone close to her. In fact, she was too big for her
environment; and it is a temptation to suggest that her
only motive in writing was to break away from it.

No such simple summary can really do justice to
Edith, who was both complex herself and hard to know.
It is true, however, that her eminence made possible a
detachment from family, husband, and country. The
world at her feet as the twentieth century opened was
European—that fascinating, exclusive, brilliant society
which then led Western culture. We cannot grudge

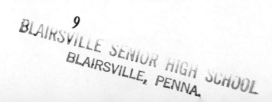

Edith a place which she honestly earned. We can only notice that she is a lonely and slightly pathetic figure in it, despite her assurance. People admired her, but she frightened them. They enjoyed her; they were dazzled; they were even fond of her; but with few exceptions, they were not intimate. Edith Wharton was one of those people who are always in control. You had to step up into her world to know her at all. She was not capable of stepping down.

Such a nature, for all its powers of perception, is essentially rigid. Edith, as critics are quick to point out, was diamond-hard. When she cut out America, or her brother Freddy, or even her husband from her life, she did not look back often with soft, nostalgic regret. When she revisited New York for the first time in many years, she said nothing of the pleasures of seeing old acquaintances. Her comment was acid. After a week in New York, she remarked, she found she was suffering from intellectual starvation. The truth is, an inner force drove Edith on which spared nobody, and least of all herself. Hard people are usually supposed not to feel. Edith Wharton was far from insensitive. She knew tenderness, love, passion, and sorrow. She was merely unable to establish an inner relationship on these terms with other people.

The consequence was an unhappy life, yet not a miserable one. Edith suffered deeply, and yet from day to day she enjoyed much. No one knew more interesting people, felt keener pleasures in books and conversations, house, travel, clothes, food, or garden. All the daily happenings of her life stimulated her. The only trouble was that she had to keep things coming, to turn her attention from one little pleasure to another, always hurrying in case some unoccupied minute should find her where she really lived inside herself, desolate and alone. Yet even here there were compensations. At peace she could never be, but out of the tensions and disquiet of her inner life, she could create. If she had established the inward happiness of which she dreamed, she might have found not more to say, but less. Completely contented, she could have submerged herself in daily life without ever thinking about human problems or values.

If Edith's unhappiness made her an interesting figure, it is her courage which made her an admirable one. Her intellect, though formidable, was limited. Her perceptions covered only a small human field. But she never gave up. Undaunted and armored in out-of-date prejudice, she advanced to tackle the twentieth century. She battered at it, and in the process of doing so, she made her own mark. We find, almost with surprise, that we respect her. She has found things to say which have some importance in the long and complex history of human society. She is not, admittedly, a literary figure of the very first rank. Nor is she one of those writers who blaze trails for others to follow. She is, however, a genuinely original creator with a personality and a view of life all her own. Edith Wharton was not an ordinary woman, and it would be impossible to judge her work by ordinary standards. She has not greatness, but brilliance. It is a quality almost as uncommon, almost as interesting; and it possesses a survival value of its own. Edith Wharton is still worth reading and widely read. It seems probable that she will remain so when more significant figures are gathering dust on the shelf. But the twentieth century goes on its way undisturbed by her intrusion. She never succeeded in imposing a shape on that.

EDITH WHARTON

1862–1937

Chapter 1

THE WORLD
OF LITTLE MISS JONES

NEW YORK in the eighteen-forties was still essentially
the New York of the American Revolution. Mighty
changes, though impending, were unforeseen. The flood
of immigration from Europe was so far a mere trickle.
Great industrial fortunes were not yet being controlled
or spent in New York. Leading citizens still belonged
to the old Dutch families, intermingled with newcomers
of middle-class British stock. Their wealth was still mer-
cantile. With the growth of the nation, their moderate
incomes had increased to considerable ones. By the
eighteen-forties their commercial energies were conse-
quently tailing off. The narrow limits of Manhattan and
the demands of a growing city were producing a fantastic spiral in real estate values. It was becoming too
easy for a man to live on his inherited fortune if it included tracts of Manhattan land. Banking and trade lost

interest for people who could live luxuriously and let their wealth pile itself up unassisted. New York society, a little inbred, a little snobbish, a little inclined to pride itself on its Dutch blood and its position for the past two hundred years, was almost beginning to think mere money-getting beneath it. At all events, the well-bred did not discuss the subject.

Such attitudes are often superficial. Blue family blood and even excellent breeding have small chance in society without money. Mary Stevens Rhinelander had been left a widow with four children before she was thirty. Being a woman, she had received no education in the management of affairs larger than her own household. Money matters were entirely in the hands of her brother-in-law. Mary Rhinelander's guardian prospered, but her own fortune diminished. It became necessary for her to sell the New York house and retire with her children to the country place looking out across Hell Gate. Here she brought up her family in genteel poverty which included private tutors, riding horses, a conservatory, chilblains, homemade dresses, and deprivation of their proper social milieu. Lucretia, her eldest daughter, made her debut in her mother's white satin slippers, which did not fit and were agony to dance in. Lucretia, though not a beauty, had style. The humiliation of those slippers, and perhaps of the homemade dress, had really rankled. Not surprisingly, she fell in love with a nice young man who could afford to see that such mortifications should never beset her again. Lucretia's feelings were genuine enough, but her temperament was thoroughly matter-of-fact. By great good fortune, the suitable young man returned her attachment.

George Frederic Jones was nineteen at this time and a handsome young man with regular features, bright blue eyes, high color, and dark brown hair which he wore long over the ears, as was the fashion. His father had a town house and a country house, the latter where Eighty-second Street is now, looking out across the East River. Communications by boat between Eighty-second Street and Hell Gate were quite easy. The Joneses, however, were not in favor of the match. Lucretia Rhinelander was little more than a poor relation, though of unexceptionable birth and breeding. George Frederic was told to forget her, and his father cut off communications by refusing to let the boy have a sailboat. In the idiom of that day and of that group, this was equivalent to a modern well-to-do father's refusing a car. It was just about as successful. George got up early, took out his rowboat, rigged up a sail from his bed quilt, and sped off to do his courting. This spirited conduct seems to have brought his father round. A year later, when George was twenty and his Lou but nineteen, the two were married.

The young Jones couple set up housekeeping in Gramercy Park with nothing to do but enjoy themselves and perform the complicated duties of formal calls, dining out, entertaining in style, and acquiring a country place in which to spend the summer. George had no profession and subsisted on a generous allowance from his father. His outdoor sports were sailing, shooting, and fishing. In a mild way he was a gourmet and became a good judge of wine. It is difficult to tell what he did with his day or what he really was interested in. The enterprise he had shown in his courtship seemed to have died out under intimate contact with the prosaic spirit of his bride. Lucretia, though by nature an indolent girl, had her household to manage and her twin passions to gratify —for clothes and for the social life which had been hitherto beyond her reach. She was satisfied with the course of events, and presently family cares took up her time. She bore two sons, Frederic and Henry.

If George Jones could be said to have a passion, it was certainly for travel. He was never a great reader, but when he did open a book, it would almost invariably be some traveler's tale. In particular, he read whatever came out on Arctic exploration. His early marriage had ended any ambitions he might have had to seek adventure. Such travel, however, as was possible with a wife and family, a nurse, a personal maid, perhaps a male attendant, was still within his powers. The young couple had honeymooned in Cuba; and as soon as it was possible to travel after the birth of their oldest child, they set out for Europe. Visits to Europe were distinctly fashionable in those days. New York society crossed the ocean fre-

quently in the new passenger steamers. People met one
another in Paris or Rome or Cannes. They did not mix
often with the natives of these parts, being too conscious
of their breeding to make friends with the middle class
and too haughty to push their way at the court of the
king of France—a dull fellow—or even at that of the
young British queen, Victoria. It was painfully obvious
that European aristocrats had no conception of the difference between the genuine families of old New York
and the shoddy imitations with far too much money and
intolerable manners who were already beginning to in-
sert themselves into better society than would receive
them at home. Disdaining these vulgarities, New Yorkers kept themselves to themselves and mainly met one
another. Yet for all their pride in their breeding, they
did not travel for love of art or any deep understanding
of European treasures. They came quite literally to see
the world. They gaped at waterfalls and picturesque
nooks such as they might have enjoyed without crossing
the Atlantic. They trundled in stuffy and uncomfortable
coaches through cobbled medieval streets. They rented
chilly Venetian palaces, impressed by the magnificence
of their surroundings, but uncritical of the cosy hideousness of their own homes in New York. They stared at
Raphael, preferring art well rounded, in perspective,
and above all decently clothed. They watched proces-
sions and fiestas—all the colorful pomp of old kingdoms
or of the Catholic church. Without really joining in the

life of the old world, they let it unroll before their fascinated eyes. Narrow quarters on steamships, hours in railway stations, jolting, horse-drawn coaches, and dingy overnight stops were not too expensive a price to pay for such a crowded pageant.

It was really sporting of Lucretia Jones to indulge her husband's restlessness when encumbered by a twenty-month-old baby. In fact, it was actually rash. These were days before typhoid shots, pasteurized milk, or sanitary drainage. Little Freddy was ill enough to make his parents somewhat regret their imprudence. Happily, all ended well. In 1847–48, the Joneses wintered in Paris, which was to Lucretia the highlight of her tour. In Paris, there were shops.

She looked well in clothes, since she had a beautiful carriage and the lovely sloping shoulders fashionable then. Extravagance was surely permissible on one's first Paris visit. Lucretia bought elegant dresses with low shoulders and wide ruffled collars. She bought tippets of ermine, carved fans, a taffeta cloak, and a wonderful bonnet of white satin decorated with dangling crystal pendants. Crinolines did not come in till 1853, but clothes were moving from the high-waisted clinging styles of the first Napoleon to the voluminous draperies and richer fabrics of the Second Empire. History was moving on, too, at an even faster pace than Paris fashions. While Lucretia was satisfying her soul with clothes, revolution broke out.

Eighteen-forty-eight is known in Europe as the year of revolutions. All of them started from Paris. All were the upsurge of a liberal, romantic, passionate outburst against the outmoded monarchies of Europe. Eighteen-forty-eight was a year of pure idealism, vast emotion, self-sacrifice, martyrdom, and disillusion. To the Joneses, it was merely another part of the pageant they were watching. When the actress Rachel broke into the "Marseillaise" and the whole audience rose to sing it with her, George commented in his journal that her passion was "rather overacted." Lucretia's memory retained the thrill of watching from the window of her hotel the flight of King Louis-Philippe. A very stout elderly gentleman with a pointed head (often portrayed by cartoonists as an animated pear on legs) went trotting anxiously across the Tuileries gardens, hurrying with him his equally undistinguished queen in the direction of a cab lurking at a back gate. The excitement of the moment was heightened by memories of the past. A previous king to run away from the Paris mob had been Louis XVI, who had been caught, brought back, and guillotined. History did not repeat itself this time, but the scene had a tension which made it a high point of the great European show displayed for Lucretia. Any connection between revolutionary ideals and the founding principles of the great American republic simply escaped her.

Kindly and harmless, just as they had left New York,

the Joneses returned. Perhaps they were dressed up a little in their Paris clothes and enlarged views of the world, but the people inside these ornaments were still the same. They settled back into New York, which was beginning to expand at an unprecedented rate. Presently they moved up to Twenty-third Street as the town grew. Old Mr. Jones died and left a handsome fortune, which may have encouraged them to branch out further. Northern Manhattan was becoming cluttered with makeshift wooden shanties, tethered goats, piles of rubbish, ragged children. The country houses in these parts were being abandoned. Steamboats now ran up and down the coast, making Newport a comfortable overnight trip. There was already a summer colony there of wealthy Southerners come up to get cool breezes. Bostonians and New Yorkers were joining them. George and Lou established themselves at Pencraig, a large house typical of the period, crisscrossed with painted beams, its roof displaying a bewildering array of points and gables. Wide verandahs, festooned with clematis and honeysuckle, surrounded the living rooms which were cool and dark. There could be dogs here or ponies for the boys. When they grew older, there would be a catboat each and plenty of sailing. There would be no question of their going to school anywhere, so they could easily spend a long summer here with their tutor. New York life with its rituals of calling and of daily afternoon drives moved up for Lou.

It seems just possible that George was aware of an emptiness behind the façade of his life, but he did nothing; and when the Civil War came, he took no part. He was nearly forty by then and apparently not rugged. He was on the board of one or two charities but had no experience in administration which could have been much use. Perhaps also, devoted husband as he was, he felt concerned for Lou, who after many years was once more pregnant. On January 24, 1862, she bore a daughter whom they called Edith Newbold Jones. The Newbold family, connected by friendship and also by the marriage of Lucretia's younger sister Mary, was one of New York's best. No doubt Lucretia with her intensely feminine tastes rejoiced in a girl. The proud father and the brothers, big boys by now, were clearly delighted.

Such was the little world of Edith Jones. The name of Edith was not thought appropriate for the pet of so many elders. She was called Pussy from the first. We catch a glimpse of her at the age of four, a chubby, rosy little girl in a marvelous bonnet of white satin patterned with pink and green plaid in raised velvet and thickly ruffled with blonde lace under the brim, the whole surmounted by a veil of white lacy wool to protect her cheeks from the cold. Her handsome father was taking her for a walk down the cobbled street which was then Fifth Avenue, running between forbidding rows of low brownstone houses. Of course they met a family friend. Pussy knew who he was, but he stood outside her real world, which at present consisted of a tall father, a lovely, scented mother, two jolly brothers, the older now at college, and—more familiar and more loved— Doyley her nurse, and a little white spitz puppy. Of the village which was New York to her parents—Washington Square, Fourteenth Street, West Twenty-third, she had small impression. Before it could fix itself indelibly on her mind, her life was to change.

During the Civil War a great many people made money in New York, but these were the thrusters and gamblers—war profiteers, early industrialists, newspaper proprietors. Gentlemen at leisure found no opportunities in these eventful times. Fixed incomes were gradually lessened by currency depreciation. By the end of the conflict, George Jones's fortune was considerably contracted. It had become evident that he could no longer go on living in his accustomed style. Meanwhile, the cost of the social round in New York was steadily rising. The town by now was very nearly a million and firmly established as the business center of the country. Great fortunes were being rapidly made by people appearing from upstate New York or from the Middle West. They were being almost as rapidly spent. Leonard Jerome, American grandfather of Winston Churchill, was one of these speculators and typical of his kind. A music lover, he built himself a private opera house. A passionate devotee of horse racing, he owned fantastic stables paneled, carpeted, and lighted with plate glass.

His "diamond dinner" in the great ballroom of Delmonico's restaurant was deliberately designed as the most expensive feast ever hitherto staged in New York. Blue-blood society both could and did ignore Jerome vulgarities, but all the same, it had to retain its position at the top of the social heap by offering something. French chefs, private balls, extravagant jewels were beginning to be commonplace in social circles. The Joneses in the difficult postwar years could not afford them.

It was cheaper to live in Europe in spite of the nearness of Paris shops, in spite of the nurse and the tutors, the maids, and the travel. The rental of properties in Newport and New York in fashionable quarters could realize large sums. The cost of entertaining abroad would be small, since social contacts were bound to be restricted. Prudence, and perhaps a last fling of the adventurous spirit, suggested travel. Pretty soon little Edith's world was transferred to Rome. She found herself playing with suitable American children in the gardens of historic villas or strolling with her parents on the Palatine hill, where it was then the fashion to gather up broken bits of lapis lazuli, porphyry, or marble from the ruins of Nero's Golden House to make inlaid tables or other bits of drawing-room adornment. The memories of four are short, and Edith's recollections of New York had faded into mist. From the first, however, she formed a clearer picture of her new surroundings than she had done of the old. Rome spoke to her in a fresh way, not merely because she was older, but because what she saw was now harmonious and beautiful. It had not yet dawned on George and Lou that their daughter was not the sweet little doll that they presumably expected. Yet apparently at this very early age the first beginnings of a lifelong passion for beauty and art became established.

It had by no means been George Jones's intention to move from New York merely to establish himself quietly in Rome. He had no occupation there, and presently the sights which it afforded his gaze became familiar. He had seen the heavy coaches of cardinals flashing in scarlet and gold through dark, narrow streets. He had been dazzled by the myriad candles and the clouds of golden incense at high mass in St. Peter's. He had watched the Carnival procession showered with blossoms. He was used to the splendor and the squalor which were the contrasting sides of Papal Rome, and he craved new scenes. After a few months' residence, he set out with Lou and his little daughter to tour Spain.

It was a real adventure like their first European trip with little Freddy. Spain had not moved with the times. The railway ran only to Madrid, and after that they were on their own. Tourists were unexpected and ill provided for. As an old woman, Edith recalled a confused memory of the bells of the *diligence*, the cracking of whips, the yells of gaunt muleteers hurling stones at gaunter mules to get them up precipitous slopes, of coming late and hungry to squalid, flea-ridden inns, finding nothing suitable for a little girl to eat but chocolate and olives, making their way through touts, guides, deformed beggars, catching glimpses of Cordova, the Alhambra, and the Escorial. Luckily for her parents, she behaved better than her brother Freddy and did not fall ill. By the end of the year, the Joneses were settled comfortably in Paris for the winter.

Little Edith was five by this time and had already begun to develop along unexpected lines. Her mother was anxious to provide playmates of her own age and a suitable sort, but the life they were leading made this far from easy. Necessarily Edith learned to play by herself, and she had become practiced at what was really rather a remarkable game. For it she needed a book. She could not read yet and was only particular that it be a book with thick black type crowded onto the page. She opened it and began to walk up and down, turning the pages at about a reading speed. This particular combination of actions seemed to set her imagination loose; and as she walked, she told herself stories. They were never fanciful ones about fairies or animals that talked, but always about people of the sort that she herself knew . . . tall fathers, graceful mothers, boys and girls, dear nurses perhaps. These had the sorts of adventures that they really might have had, yet they definitely were not the real people. Her game was called "making up," and its fascination lay in Edith's use of her creative powers.

The little girl only played "making up" when she was alone, but she talked about it and made no secret of what she did. Curious grownups, peeping through the crack of a door, could watch her at it. They did so in amusement and pride at her quickness—at any rate at first. It would be interesting to know what Lucretia felt when the first pleasures of "making up" deepened into a sort of infantile passion. Every so often, Edith felt she had to do it, even at moments which were not quite convenient. She would come wailing to her mother, who had provided some small companion to play with. "Mamma, Mamma! You must go and entertain that little girl for me! I've got to make up!" And Edith would vanish.

With such a use for books, Edith had not much incentive for actually learning to read. She learned the alphabet reluctantly and slowly from her father. Shortly afterwards, however, she was discovered sitting under a table with a book in her lap quite evidently not "making up," since this game involved walking. Questioned, she remarked that she was reading the book. Incredulous grownups challenged her at once. She responded by actually reading a line or two. It was then discovered that the book in question was a copy of a rather scandalous play about a "certain type of woman" which was having a run in Paris. Poor Lucretia, whose girlhood had been forbidden Walter Scott, was distinctly taken aback. She need not have worried. Her daughter's experience was not on a par with her imagination. Some years later when she was back in New York, Edith formed an impression, which must have lasted for some time, that adultery had something to do with higher costs in travel. She had happened to read a sign on a ferry which said: Children a quarter. Adults fifty cents. In the absence of any explanation of a subject, she was not afraid to jump to a conclusion.

Paris became their winter home for some years. Edith at about seven was promoted to dancing classes with an elderly retired *danseuse*, very formidable looking with a perceptible mustache on her lip. The little girl was miserably trying to do graceful things with a scarf or castanets and becoming conscious that she was dreadfully shy. Her upbringing among older people had conspired to make her so. Besides, nobody shared her peculiar passions, and this threw her in on herself. About this time, however, she gained an audience.

Mary Stevens "Grandmamma" Rhinelander came to Paris for the winter. In appearance she was the conventional grandmother of the time, complete with neat lace cap and dangling sidepieces, black silk dress, gold watch chain, and fitted out with a japanned ear trumpet. Edith had discovered poetry by this time, and she wanted to hear it aloud. Since nobody read to her, she passionately desired to read it herself. Nobody in the family wanted to listen. George's knowledge of English poetry was more or less confined to Macaulay. Lucretia may possi-

bly have been exposed to elegant verses of a complimen-
tary or religious type, but in general she had no poetry
in her. A deaf grandmother with an infinite quantity of
fine sewing always at hand was a perfect solution. Little
Edith sat for hours shouting Tennyson down the ear
trumpet. Long narrative poems about King Arthur or
Lord Burleigh were not always understandable to Edith,
aged seven. But she liked the sound of them and made
up meanings for phrases as they were needed. Grandmamma may or may not have heard. At all events, she
provided sympathy for something which the child was
learning already to conceal. Edith was not ashamed of
her talents or encouraged to be so. Quite the contrary.
Yet other people so easily got bored with them.

In 1870 when Edith was eight, the Franco-Prussian
War broke out. Summer had come, and the Joneses
were no longer in Paris. They had gone to Bad Wildbad
in the Black Forest, a primitive German watering place
just coming into fashion. Prudently they stayed where
they were and missed the campaigning, which all took
place in France. Edith, however, fell desperately ill with
typhoid. It then transpired that all the local doctors had
been drafted with the exception of a senile old man who
had never before come across a case of typhoid and had
no idea what to do with it. He attempted to treat Edith
by sending notes to his son, who was with the Prussian
forces, and waiting for a reply before he did anything.
The little girl's temperature soared to shocking heights,

and it became clear that she was at the point of death. The desperate Lucretia discovered at the last minute that a well-known doctor had been summoned from Russia to treat a Russian prince at the watering place. He was in a hurry to get back and had no time for more than a flying visit, but he told the agonized mother to plunge Edith into an icy bath and bring her temperature down. At the thought of the shock to the sick child's system, Lucretia recoiled. She compromised by wrapping her in wet sheets and was successful. Edith lived, but was delicate for a year or two. They took her to Italy and tried to prevent her from using her brain, having the impression that overwork in that department might produce another fever. Meanwhile, George Jones's affairs in New York were prospering. His economies had been timely, and the country was recovering from the Civil War. In 1872, when Edith was ten, the family returned.

They settled back into the old brownstone, and Edith's impression was of the gloom and hideousness of New York. Surely some more handsome material than the brownstone could have been occasionally used. Public buildings were largely non-existent still, while the harbor down at the Battery, the commercial quarters, and the fringe of shanty-town had been constructed haphazardly and without regard for anything but speed and cheapness. It was depressing. Perhaps the Jones furnishings were depressing too. The current fashion called for three layers of curtain at the window, mighty furniture, and a general impression of gloomy magnificence. Lucretia's drawing room, for instance, was upholstered in purple satin with tassels and fringes of gold. It was curtained in purple velvet. It must have been quite a sight, affording a striking contrast to the airy rooms and faded hangings of Florence or Rome. However, none of these things was important to Edith in the face of one miraculous advantage which had never before come her way. George Jones had a library.

It was not much of a library, merely a gloomy room containing a fireplace with a heavy oak mantel supported by a pair of knight's heads in helmet and visor. It contained about eight hundred volumes disposed in low oak bookcases fronted with glass. These consisted pretty much of George's share of his father's library plus a few more modern sets of historical works. However, there were classical books in French and English, history, poetry, drama, essays, eighteenth-century novels. Poor Edith, though she adored her German governess, was strictly forbidden since her illness to memorize anything at all or to prepare her lessons. She fell on the library with the eagerness of someone coming into her own.

Lucretia Jones was really beginning to find little Puss a problem. Wherever she got this habit of reading from, Lucretia did not know. It was most troublesome because children's books—*Little Women*, for instance—were vulgar and made use of slipshod expressions her daughter must not pick up. Adult novels, on the other hand, even classical ones, might treat of subjects unsuitable for a young girl. Lucretia was lazy and she had not the habit of reading. It was unthinkable that she should plow through every volume Edith opened.

She solved the problem by decreeing that any novel which her daughter desired to read must be submitted to her for permission. She always refused it. In a later generation this simple method of control would not have worked, but Edith was completely absorbed by her family. She never went to school. She had not, because of her wandering life, many friends of her age. She had no opportunity to experience the divided authority which modern children learn in nursery school. She did not pick up naughtiness from playmates, was never exposed to other people's influence through radio, movies or television. The consequence was she was obedient in a literal fashion which would be inconceivable these days in any little girl of normal spirit. She put the forbidden books carefully back on the shelf and turned instead to non-fiction.

George Jones, meanwhile, was still on his charitable boards, while Lucretia had her ladies' sewing circle during Lent. No doubt it was proper to interest young girls in charitable works. Accordingly, about three years after the family's return, Miss Evelyn Washburne, daughter of the rector of Calvary Church, received a contribution from a Miss E. N. Jones in the form of an outfit for the child of a needy missionary. Miss Jones was not a parishioner and was quite unknown to Miss Washburne, who paid a call to thank her in person. Her effort was unsuccessful. Mrs. Jones, the butler stated firmly, was not at home. Miss E. N. Jones in person flashed out to make a protest, but the butler was adamant. He knew his duty. Little girls of thirteen did not receive callers.

Miss Washburne retired defeated; but her respectability was obvious and Mrs. Jones permitted the acquaintance. The two girls met and discovered a common interest in studying German. Edith, though the younger, was far the quicker and had the advantage of her German governess. Evelyn did not know what to make of her. Except when her hair was being brushed, Edith never seemed to study. Yet she embarked on Middle High German and was eager to practice on the Washburnes' typewriter. Presently the girls put their heads together over a translation of German verse which they sent in to a magazine and actually had printed. Evelyn obligingly covered up for Edith by signing her name and receiving the check, but they split the money. The work, as Evelyn admits, was mainly Edith's. Theirs was a companionship which did not lead to any lifelong friendship because they did not have very much in common. But it tided Edith over a difficult time. When Evelyn discovered that her friend was not allowed to read Goethe, she went to Mrs. Jones. Lucretia, delighted to have anyone so perfectly staid to overlook her daughter's reading, gave blanket permission for her to have any book that Evelyn chose. The German governess fed them both on the glory of the German romantics. Thus, under the mask of a sweet little girl with proper manners, pretty clothes, and suitable connections, Edith Jones's nature grew.

She had started to write soon after the return to New York. Her very first effort was the beginning of a novel which, like the stories of "making up," had its feet firmly on the ground of Edith's particular world. It commenced, with a mature sense for effect, with dialogue. " 'Oh, how do you do, Mrs. Brown?' said Mrs. Tompkins. 'If only I had known you were going to call, I should have tidied up the drawing room.' "

Trembling with the excitement of her first literary creation, Edith could not resist taking this to her mother. Literary criticism was not Lucretia's line, but it chanced that this particular offering was within her range. "Drawing rooms," she said with icy reproof, "are always tidy." It was absolutely crushing. Poor Edith abandoned her novel in utter despair and turned to poetry.

George and Lou, it is fair to say, were proud of their daughter's talents insofar as they understood them. They did not, however, consider self-expression a particularly important part of education. Edith's business was to become an attractive young girl. Harmless enjoyments were permitted as a matter of course, but need not be indulged. If the child wanted to scribble poetry, well and good. But to go out deliberately and buy her writing paper for the purpose was sheer nonsense. It gradually became understood that Edith's prerogative was all the wrapping paper that came into the house. She smoothed it out, and never thinking to cut it into pages, got down on the floor on her hands and knees and writing in columns, covered it from end to end with poetic dramas, epics, and shorter occasional poems. The invaluable governess gave her a work on prosody, and presently Edith ventured to dispatch a little poem to the editor of a newspaper. She accompanied it by a note apologizing for the irregular meter and explaining that she was a very little girl and that she liked irregular lines. The editor, a good man, replied promptly that he liked them too; and he printed the poem.

Edith went on pouring out verses, varying them with a couple of novels dripping with beautiful sentiments, for one of which she made up imaginary reviews tearing it to pieces. When she was sixteen a modest little book of her verse was privately printed in Newport, containing about two dozen poems, among them three very creditable translations from the German. Though clever, Edith's poetry did not show original merit. In fact, she had a teen-age capacity for wallowing in emotions which she had not experienced firsthand. Notwithstanding, she possessed a remarkable gift for self-expression, especially considering that some of the verse was written when she was only thirteen. The author's name was not printed, but such things are never secret. Edith proudly inscribed her own copy with a couplet:

Who wrote these verses, she this volume owns.
Her unpoetic name is Edith Jones.

In later life, Edith did not like to mention these verses; and in her memoirs she was at pains to imply that they did not exist. This has naturally led to speculation about who encouraged her to publish and paid the expenses. Possibly her father did, but it seems quite probable that it was one of her brothers. It may have been Freddy, who was already married to an attractive, vivacious girl who shared Edith's tastes. In any case, one of her brothers did show some of her efforts to a Boston friend, who passed them on to the aging Henry Wadsworth Longfellow. He in turn sent them to the *Atlantic*, where they were printed in 1880. By this time, their author had already come out and was absorbed in the social occupations of a young girl of her class. They did not create a sensation, and she was happy to have the whole episode forgotten. Writing poetry was no way to social success. It had already become an adolescent phase which she had outgrown.

During this time, while Edith's inner nature was developing on its own lines, her outer appearance as a proper young girl was being molded. In her consciousness at the time there was little conflict between these two sides of herself. She shared Lucretia's interest in clothes and felt a real thrill at helping to unpack the big boxes of marvelous dresses which were shipped to her mother every six months from Paris. When Aunt Mary Newbold asked her what she would like to be when she was grown up, her response was immediate: "The best-dressed woman in New York!"

"Oh, don't say that, darling!" cried Aunt Mary, horrified. Though prettier than her sister Lucretia, she was much more serious-minded.

"Well, but Auntie," protested the little girl in surprise, "you know, Mamma *is!*"

Edith herself was never beautiful. Her face was too long and her jaw too dominant. But she had regular features, brown eyes, and bright red hair which later darkened and made her distinctly more than passably pretty. She adored her father and growing up in a household which she hardly ever left, she took for granted the kind of life he led. In the season, George and Lou attended the opera once a week. They were not musical, but society went. They sat in a box. One listened in silence during the solos, talked under cover of the choruses, and paid calls in the intervals on other boxes. Attendance at the theater was not a social obligation. The Joneses seldom made the effort to go.

Other nights in the week they dined out or gave dinners. These varied in size and formality. The most splendid required engraved invitations three weeks in advance, while the menu featured soups both thick and clear, a Roman punch halfway through the meal, and expensive delicacies such as canvasback ducks. The Joneses had a Negro cook instead of a French chef, but the cook was an artist. When Lucretia bowed to the lady on George's right and led the procession up the red velvet stairs to the purple-and-gold drawing room, the men remaining at table could look forward to a wine from one of New York's best private cellars.

They did not drink deep. It was a temperate society and the conversation was temperate too. Untouched by the roaring life of the expanding city, by literature, philosophy, art, even by politics, men discussed the selection of copper beeches for their country places, talked over their horses or their plans for European travel. If none of these themes had any novelty in them, they turned to food or wine, inexhaustible subjects. It was all very pleasant, polite, and a little static. It suited a society in which, when the host turned from the lady on his right to converse with the one on his left, every gentleman about his board followed suit—never too much interested in what he was saying to break it off. In more intimate dinners, to be sure, conversation was freer; but it never scaled heights.

This kind of social life took up the time of George and Lou in New York fairly completely. It was not merely that such dinners involved planning, that invitations were written by hand when not engraved and were seldom entrusted to the mail. Purchasing, especially of meat, presented problems unknown to the age of the freezer. An army of servants, and perhaps a few extra hired ones, had to be managed. It was not merely drudgery of this sort which kept the Joneses busy. In a society where the men were unemployed or at the most visited a legal office mainly out of form, the social season extended itself to lunch. This in its turn increased the number of necessary calls.

Calls were paid after every party of every description and on special At Home days, which ladies adopted presumably to insure their ever being at home to their own callers. Important family events brought further calls. Armed with their cardcases, the ladies, on whom a great many of these duties fell, spent their afternoons leaving cards on friends and going in, if the hostess were at home, for a strict half hour. Cards were turned down in the upper lefthand corner if the caller had asked to see the lady of the house and not merely handed her card to the servant and retired. Congratulations or condolence were signified by other corners. The purpose of this shorthand was not to inform the hostess what your call was about, which she could learn from her servant. The cards were intended for display in the front hall to show newcomers what people had already done the polite thing. So demanding were these ceremonies that Edith scarcely ever saw her mother go out in the daytime without her cardcase in her hand.

All this was life as the grownups lived it. Edith's brothers, grown men by now, partook of it too. To be sure, Harry's life as a bachelor about town was much gayer, but the pattern was the same. In Newport, Edith shared it more intimately. Harry was a particularly popular young man. Young people of both sexes crowded Pencraig. There was much laughter. Archery meetings, sailing parties, and picnics were the order of the day.

The little girl had loved Pencraig from the first. It was such a relief after New York to scamper in a daisied meadow, to drink in the colors of the ocean and the rocks, the sharp contours of the land. She still had to play by herself. There was a pony, but her father and the boys never rode. She had to go with the groom and keep to the hard roads. In fact, she never became particularly at home on a horse.

She never cared for sailing either. It took concentration just when she wanted to relax and drink in the scene. She joined, however, in her brothers' swimming parties. Archery meets were the favorite mixed sports of those days. They suited the costumes of the girls, still rather encumbering for tennis. Little girls, not precisely invited, were welcome to wander and stare. Informal picnics were always being arranged, and Edith was included as a matter of course among the Joneses. It occurred to nobody, least of all to Edith herself, that she ought to be shunted off with her own age level. Outside the life of the family, she was dreadfully shy.

Society in Newport had been steadily changing while
Edith was growing up. Wealthy Southerners had dis-
appeared with the Civil War. There was a colony of
Bostonians, some of them quite distinguished; but they
held aloof. The bulk of the summer residents were coming from New York. In fact, the extraordinary scramble
to get "in" to society which was taking place in New
York was transferred in summer to Newport. Families
were beginning to try to outbuild one another. Liveried
servants, costly decorations, vast entertainments were
becoming the rule. Nor were these confined by any
means to new arrivals who aspired to get to the top.
Ward MacAllister, a genial bachelor who had managed
to set himself up as the social arbiter in New York, was
putting luxurious touches into what had originally been
quite simple picnics. His method was to ask each lady
guest what her cook's best dish might be, and to tell her
to bring it. Young men were taxed a bottle of champagne, a supply of grapes, or ice cream. MacAllister
rented a suitable local farm for the day, instructed the
farmer to dress his family in holiday clothes, sent out a
carpenter to put up a dancing platform, and a florist to
ornament it. Musicians and servants followed. The party
met on Narragansett Avenue in a cluster of handsome
four-in-hands or tandems, and drove out to the spot.
The band struck up a waltz while the champagne was
disposed in ice and the various dishes arranged on al
fresco tables. A banquet followed, and afterwards there

was more dancing. MacAllister spared no pains to produce perfection, even hiring a flock of sheep on one occasion together with two yoke of oxen to give his own summer place "an animated appearance."

These picnics at least must have been a good deal of fun. But the routines of calling and turning down the corners of cards were just as demanding as they had been in New York. The afternoon parade seems equally dull. Every day the older ladies in brocaded dresses powerfully boned, small flower-trimmed bonnets, tulle veils, and holding fringed silk sunshades, drove solemnly up and down Bellevue Avenue in their victorias or barouches with their footmen up behind them. Younger ladies were driven by younger gentlemen in frock coats, tall hats, and pearl-gray trousers. Older men had phaetons and pairs with grooms sitting upright behind with folded arms. All these equipages passed up and down Bellevue Avenue in double lines. The first time one passed an acquaintance, one made a graceful bow. The second time, one gently nodded. The third time, one looked the other way, pretending not to have noticed.

Such rituals became more and more demanding. As Edith grew older, she was drawn into them at her mother's side. Not being out yet, she was spared the formal entertainments, but picnics were more all-embracing. Painfully shy, she did not make a good impression.

Prominent among the Bostonians who spent their summers at Newport was Julia Ward Howe, distinguished authoress. While the New Yorkers were establishing the routines of their set, Mrs. Howe had founded a club to prevent the waste of summers by arranging improving lectures from prominent people who happened to be in Newport. Julia had been a New Yorker herself, but she had married a well-known Boston philanthropist of obscure background and was seen no more in New York. Her brother, however, was a genial man-about-town much in society. Julia's daughters had a certain claim on attention. They happened to be pretty. It followed that though they lived in a plebeian way, associating with distinctly cranky people, they were occasionally asked to MacAllister's parties or other such entertainments. Though quite a bit older than "Pussy" Jones, they met her and summed her up as a haughty, stuck-up girl who was as cold as ice. The atmosphere in the Howe household was particularly warm. Julia was affectionate and sentimental as well as intelligent. She and her children had the habit of pouring out light verse to celebrate family occasions. The Howe girls, slightly out of things, despised the fashionable life of the resort, and felt it despised them. In return, they prided themselves on their superior culture and poetic skill. It was really a rude shock when that silent, supercilious little Pussy published her poems. They could not understand it. Edith's achievement did not endear her to them, and they refrained from any attempt to break the ice.

They would not have succeeded. Shyness and arrogance are a formidable combination. In Edith's case, they were two sides of the same thing. She was trying to keep people away from her real self. By upbringing, and indeed by nature, she had plenty of assurance. The aristocrat is taught to look down on ordinary people and not to be afraid to be rude when occasion demands it. But with her equals, Edith felt stiff and nervous, never certain that she would really fit in. She was anxious to do so, not yet questioning the standards of her world; but she felt inadequate. It had not yet become apparent to her that she felt bored.

Chapter 2

MISS JONES MAKES
HER DEBUT

EDITH's parents decidedly did not want a bluestocking daughter. At seventeen she was beginning to absorb her brothers' college texts in a desperate quest for solid intellectual food. It was somewhat early to bring a girl out, but the experience would take her mind off books. How to do it was a problem. Coming-out parties, like every other social event in New York, were becoming an excuse for a bewildering extravagance. Even in the matter of dinners, the Joneses could not keep up with private banqueting halls, a service of gold plate, or the vast entertainments people staged at Delmonico's. Wisely, they had not attempted to. New York's upper crust in 1879 was maintaining its position—or its less wealthy members were doing so—by cultivating a reputation for exclusiveness. The Four Hundred, as they had come to be nicknamed, had their own subscription balls—the

Patriarchs' and the Family Circle Dancing Class for young married couples and debs. The right of entry to these guaranteed a position which roused envy in everyone else. Other large-scale entertainments were falling into the hands of the millionaires. Gradually the circle of the elect was being forced open to include numbers of these, since otherwise they might set up their own society and bypass the older group. Yet the larger the proportion of the very wealthy became, the more unreal the position of George and Lou and their friends turned out to be. It was all very well for them to look down on extravagance and call it vulgar. They were now part of a set which had invented the costume ball as an excuse for thousand-dollar costumes for the men and even more expensive ones for the ladies. Without knowing it, George and Lou were being reduced to parasites in the small New York village which was theirs by right of inheritance. They were conferring little but the honor of their presence on the social scene. Still sought after, they were not aware of these sad facts; but the problem of how to bring Edith out became apparent.

With her usual practical sense, Lucretia decided that to give a big party was nonsense. Why present Pussy in a formal way when the people she was meeting were all old family friends who knew her already? It was quite sufficient to introduce her at a small private ball of somebody else's.

In this inexpensive way, therefore, Miss Edith Jones

was launched. Her mother chose her a dress with a green brocade bodice to set off her reddish-brown hair and a white skirt covered with ruffles of Valenciennes lace. Her hair was put up and she was given a large bouquet of lilies of the valley. One of the most horrible evenings of her career ensued. Her brothers' friends, who naturally knew her already, were very kind. But it was agony to be asked to dance, and even worse not to. She had nothing to say and felt that her awkwardness was an embarrassment to the men who took pity upon her. Happily, after the first plunge, coming out proved not too bad. There were no special debutante parties, but a great many lunch parties, or small dinners among the young married set. These always included an unmarried girl or two, and Edith's position was assured by the popularity of Harry. She began to enjoy herself as the situation and the group became familiar. When she forgot her shyness, she was quick-witted in retort and had an animation which could not fail to please. There were other dresses besides the green brocade. The satisfaction of setting off a neat figure to advantage was profound. Edith's first New York season was a gay time, too busy with little social triumphs for much reading or for writing poetry. Newport followed with fishing parties and lawn tennis played in tail coats and tight whaleboned dresses. One particular young man became very attentive, and Edith allowed herself to be pleased. Lucretia's formula for making her daughter a normal young girl appeared to have worked.

This pleasant period of life was interrupted by a mixture of sorrow and joy. George Jones's health was failing, and the doctors recommended a mild climate. He and Lucretia were going to Europe for an indefinite time, taking their daughter with them.

Edith really loved her father, but youth is hopeful. Her dreams were coming true. Ever since she was ten years old, she had been longing for Europe. What was a season in New York full of dull dinners or trivial young men? Who cared about Newport picnics or lawn tennis as compared to Venice or Rome? Edith's heart was not deeply touched, and she was so young that marriage merely presented itself as the right way to settle down. This must be some time ahead, and meanwhile—what? Had her father arranged his illness merely to please Edith, he could hardly have succeeded any better.

Europe came fully up to expectations. George Jones was not well, but he was not a complete invalid. His six years' residence abroad had by no means left him untouched by European culture. For one thing, since that first trip of his with Lou and little Freddy, the work of Ruskin had educated a whole generation of tourists in the broad outlines of Italian art. Without really studying, George had picked up a good deal. He now took considerable pleasure in passing on what he had learned to his daughter and in letting her enthusiasm lead him. George's casual, dilettante approach was insufficient for her. She had her Ruskin in her hand and dragged her father on an organized pilgrimage through all the places that Ruskin had visited in Florence and Venice. George's own initiative would never have led him to be thorough, but his pleasure in his daughter's companionship must have been deep. Unhappily the general state of his health did not improve, despite winters spent in the still milder climate of Cannes.

Lucretia probably knew that George was a dying man, but his decline over two years was gradual. Edith did not perceive that he was getting worse. To be sure, he ceased to take her about; but this was partly due to other circumstances. Two American girls of Lucretia's generation had married into the old French nobility, the group that inhabited the Faubourg St. Germain in Paris and thought themselves as exclusive in their sphere as George and Lou were in New York. These ladies both wintered in Cannes. Both had daughters quite close to Edith's age. They were delighted to take her everywhere with them and to expose her to all the pleasures of the fashionable season. Edith's shyness and reserve were giving way to other qualities more characteristic of her real self. She was one of those fortunate people who are born afresh every day with a new zest for living. In a society where she felt at home, she had a quick wit and a flashing power of repartee. Cultivated young

Frenchmen had interests akin to hers, and Edith discovered that she had a power of attracting friends of her own. Besides, somebody had followed her all the way from New York; and for a brief period Edith allowed herself to be talked into an engagement. The young man's mother was one of the new social-climbing set in New York, Mrs. Paran Stevens, wife of a big hotel operator. Such a connection would have grated on Edith's family and possibly on herself. At all events, the lovers quarreled and did not make it up. Edith's attention to her father's health, distracted by this affair, was suddenly recalled. In 1882, after a long decline, George unexpectedly collapsed and died. Lucretia and her daughter returned to New York in strict mourning. Even had Edith the heart for much diversion, it would not have been permitted for the first year. In the summer at Newport, restraints were slightly relaxed. Gradually wounds healed. Edith resumed social life, but with a difference. The Joneses were really not in the center of things.

New York social life, even in the two or three years since Edith had entered it, had become more obviously based on money. In 1883, for instance, shortly after Lucretia and her daughter had returned from Europe, occurred the incident of the famous Vanderbilt ball. Society at this time was dominated by Mrs. William Astor, who employed her millions in display of every sort and had taken over the exclusive group in which George and Lou had once moved. Looking down from these heights on other millionaires, comparative new-comers to New York, Mrs. Astor kept the barriers firmly up. The Vanderbilts, second generation merely, were vulgar. Mrs. Vanderbilt, as ambitious as Mrs. Astor and as wealthy, might build herself a palace in Newport and another in New York. She might flaunt herself in her jewels in second-rate society if she chose. A real position in the New York social world was not to be bought.

So Mrs. Astor maintained, but the facts did not bear her out. By lavish expenditures, Mrs. Vanderbilt had to a large extent found her way in. Only Mrs. Astor, who did not need to depend on other people's money, still held aloof. In 1883, the last citadel fell. Mrs. Vander-bilt's ball was to be the most splendid thing of the sea-son, a costume affair. The opportunity for extraordinary display in clothes and jewels was too tempting to be missed. All society was invited and was going—except Mrs. Astor. No card had been sent to Mrs. Astor be-cause she had never called on Mrs. Vanderbilt—in other words, did not know her. It was an awkward sit-uation. Should the queen of New York society sit at home while her attendants danced at her rival's? Mrs. Astor weighed the matter while the New York social world held its breath. Eventually, only just in time to get her own costume made, Mrs. Astor called.

After that, the ball was almost an anticlimax, though histories and novels had been ransacked for authentic

details of famous historical costumes affording opportunity to display jewelry. Mrs. Vanderbilt went as a
Venetian princess. Her sister-in-law, simpler-minded,
went as "The Electric Light" in white satin, creating
the necessary blaze with the aid of diamonds. The vast
Vanderbilt palace in a "Greek Renaissance" brownstone style was filled with treasures of European and
Japanese art, banked with flowers, and hung with pale
red velvet, lavishly embroidered with foliage and jeweled butterflies. The guests assembled for the quadrilles
on the third floor and moved down a grand stone stair-
case fifty feet high, through a hall sixty-five feet long,
and into a drawing room wainscoted with carved wal-
nut from a French château. The spectacle, perhaps the
most brilliant ever seen in New York, was a practical
demonstration of the fact that social position was now
up for sale.

The fact was noted, and entertainments became still
more lavish. In the following year a ten-thousand-dollar
banquet was given in Delmonico's ballroom for seventy-
two people. An immense oval table surrounded a bank
of flowers with a lake thirty feet long in the center,
enclosed in a network of gold wire and containing four
live swans. Songbirds in golden cages were scattered all
over the room. There was no relationship between this
sort of thing and the purple upholstery or the excellent
family cook of Lou. The quiet entertainment of old
friends was being succeeded by immense impersonal

crushes where conversation sank far below the level of quiet dullness which pervaded those earlier dinners. To be sure, the exclusive and dowdy still existed alongside the newer rich and still persisted in their old-fashioned ways. But the spirit had gone out of them. They lacked new blood. The younger generation, to which Edith Jones belonged, was exposed to their trivialities without being able to regard them as the leaders of their own world.

In this unsatisfactory way Miss Edith Jones, living quietly with her widowed mother, surveyed the social scene. Her brothers, however, had many friends. Pencraig still resounded with cheerful laughter every summer. Presently, as was to be expected, Edith fell more seriously in love.

He was not her first cavalier. Edith saw plenty of young men. Among them, a distant cousin, one Walter Van Rensselaer Berry, had impressed her with a quickness of mind and a love of books like her own. But Walter Berry had his private plans for life and his ambitions. No doubt he found the young girl unsophisticated, despite her European polish. The real Edith was still peeping timidly from beneath the maternal wing. At all events, Walter Berry went away and did not repeat his visit. Edith chose from among more familiar figures a friend of her brother.

Edward Robbins Wharton was an eligible bachelor from Boston, twelve years out of Harvard and by that much Edith's senior. He had no profession, was very much the gentleman, kindly, and without a brain in his head. He was devoted to outdoor sports, a rider, a figure skater, a fly fisherman. In appearance he was slim, not particularly tall, dressed carefully, and displayed a well-tended mustache. In sum, he was George Jones all over again, perhaps a little easier in manner, more vigorous physically, but with the same lack of ambition or intelligent interests.

It may seem extraordinary that Edith should have married such a man at twenty-three, an age when modern girls have finished college and in general have a pretty good idea what their tastes are. One can only take it as a measure of the innocence produced by her upbringing at home and the narrow society into which she had been born. It is fair to remember, also, that Edward Wharton, though no intellectual, came from an intelligent family and was used to a more cultured group than that of New York. He happened to know quite a number of interesting people and may have seemed to open a window onto a world Edith could share. Their age difference certainly gave him a sophisticated air and made her feel flattered. For the rest, he was devoted to her and always pleasant in society. People liked him. His conversation was gay and could be amusing. To pushing inferiors he was capable of an aristocratic rudeness, but his familiars remembered him for little attentions springing from real considerateness

and not mere good manners. What he saw in Edith
Jones is more understandable than what she saw in him.
Only perhaps in her first season was Edith ever a modest
little dove among other nice girls. Her real friends later
compared her to the golden pheasant or to the soaring
eagle. Teddy Wharton admired her flashing wit, her
competence, and her capacity for joy to his life's end.
What he did not from the height of his twelve extra
years perceive, was that sooner or later the gorgeous
creature would learn to use her wings and soar above
him.

Chapter 3

UNEQUAL MARRIAGE

EDITH JONES had on her father's death acquired a fortune which was held in trust for her by her brothers. Teddy Wharton had an allowance from his father. The combination of these resources promised comfort, though in a more modest way than Edith was used to. Teddy did not like Boston, and Edith under his influence thought as he did. Boston is clannish, while she was still shy with strangers. In later life she complained that in Boston she was thought too fashionable to be intelligent, whereas New Yorkers thought her too intelligent to be fashionable. There was something in this, and neither city pleased the newly-married pair. Teddy wanted to live in Newport all the year round. It suited their income, and he liked the climate. Edith really did not. Besides, she hated the formalities of the Newport season, which were still as stringent as ever. Once Edith hired a new coachman who did not know her mother; and he inadvertently passed that lady's carriage on the

daily afternoon drive on Bellevue Avenue. To kick up
the dust ahead of one's elders was an unpardonable rudeness. Edith paid a special call to explain that her coachman had had no idea what he was doing. Lucretia, still
affronted, merely remarked, "You might have told him."

For reasons of this sort, Edith did not care for Newport; but she was not sure what she did want. Lucretia
offered a smallish cottage on Pencraig grounds, a real
economy which would make it possible to spend four
months of the year in travel. Edith was wild to see more
of Italy. Teddy was willing. Thus a pattern for their
married life established itself. Edith, who had inherited
great practical gifts from her mother, expended herself
during eight months of the year in creating perfection in
the little Newport house. Perfection to Edith did not involve a light hand with pastry or an aptitude for the
drudgeries of housework. She always had maids for
these things and gardeners to do the hard work out-of-
doors. Her part in the matter consisted in planning for
comfort, in demanding and getting perfect service, and
in making all her servants happy to be with her. She had
in addition an educated good taste which grew with the
years. She took a real interest in interior decoration, in
which subject she was far in advance of her age. Likewise in gardening, she became knowledgeable about
plants and landscape design, poring endlessly over seed
and nursery catalogs, always delighted by a chance to

spend an afternoon with other experts. She and Teddy entertained a good deal in the little house, which was not really so very small according to modern ideas. Edith's window onto a larger world did open slightly as she met her husband's friends. A few of these instantly perceived that Teddy was a mere nonentity beside his Edith.

Chief among such new connections was Charles Eliot Norton, professor of fine arts at Harvard and an inspiration to a whole generation of students there. Old enough to be Edith's father, he had been less a personal than a family friend on the Wharton side. Professor Norton was a really distinguished and cultured man, probably more so than anyone Edith had hitherto met. She found him fascinating to talk to, and he seems no less to have enjoyed her. Their relationship across a barrier of age was characteristic of Edith, who combined with feminine feelings a masculine bent for intimacy on an intellectual level. She was close to Professor Norton till he died, paying him regular visits in Cambridge or in his summer place in the Berkshires.

Such were the pursuits into which Edith poured her stored energies. They were not exciting or remarkable ones, but she was in love—at the beginning at least—with a rather dull man. She was liberated from home, and the novelty of being able to do what she liked gave a sense of adventure. Apart from travel, she did not crave anything unusual. Luckily for the success of her whole marriage, Teddy, who had traveled little before, took eagerly to it.

In Teddy's case, as in that of George Jones, it is hard to tell what there was about travel which pleased him. He must have had some mild taste in art, or he could hardly have endured being dragged around by Edith. She was never content to see things in the ordinary way of a simple tourist. She wanted to study a special style or period. She wanted to explore places that were not usually seen. She taught herself by actually looking at objects what the graduate student of fine arts systematically learns today from books or lectures. In Paris, while having her portrait painted for Teddy, she accidentally saw a piece of eighteenth-century Italian furniture. It stimulated her to make a special study of that whole Italian period, which had hitherto been almost entirely neglected by specialists. Carried away by such enthusiasms, she penetrated to out-of-the-way spots, persuaded curators to open small churches or villas that were closed, made new acquaintances in Italy with a free hand. Teddy trailed after her, a thousand-dollar bill in his wallet "in case Pussy sees something." Clearly he was proud of her and spoiled her. Equally obviously, she was becoming rather used to taking the lead.

It is hard in circumstances such as these to keep up the illusion of really sharing in a marriage partnership. Accidents, however, did come to the aid of Teddy dur-

ing those early years. The first of these was the matter
of a Mediterranean cruise which was broached by a
friend of theirs, James Van Alen. Such cruises are a regular thing nowadays. In those times they were not. It
was necessary to charter a private yacht, which would
be expensive. Rumor suggested that some parts of Greece
were still infested by brigands and would be dangerous
to visit. Altogether, the thing was a considerable adventure and would cost more than the Whartons could
afford. Indeed, as Edith's indignant brothers pointed out,
it would just about swallow what the pair had to live on
for the rest of the year. As Edith's trustees and with her
interests at heart, Harry and Freddy refused to advance
any capital. Still louder outcries arose from Teddy's
family, who thought too much travel an extravagance
and that Boston was the proper place to settle down.

Taken aback, Edith hesitated. It was Teddy who said,
"The real question is, do you want to go?" Of course
Edith did! The trip was a huge success for them both,
and they returned to discover that a cousin of Edith's
had just died and left her money. Teddy's position was
doubly fortified. His daring had justified itself, while
the additional income made it possible to do other things
which Edith wanted.

Neither of them wished to admit that they were un-
suited, yet perhaps a child in these early days might have
helped. In later life, Edith's friends assert that she did
not miss children. The truth of the matter undoubtedly

is that with such enormous resources developing inside herself, she did not need to make a tragedy of being childless. Denied what she must normally have expected, she turned her creative powers to something else. The loss was not vital to her life, though it must have been felt. It may have been vital to her marriage.

Increase in income staved off discontent for a time by creating more things to do. Edith and Teddy bought a larger house in Newport, an ugly, wooden place with a fine view of the Atlantic and an acre of rocky land. Edith plunged into redecoration plans. A circular court was created with high hedges and niches of trelliswork. A young Boston architect called Ogden Codman, Jr., was hired to alter the place. He and Edith agreed that interior decoration was too often left to the upholsterer, who had no knowledge of interior design and was merely anxious to produce an expensive effect. Ogden Codman was added to the growing list of Edith's friends, and at some point or other the suggestion was thrown out that the two of them might collaborate on a book. Meanwhile, however, in spite of the European tours which still continued, in spite of the plans and the activities in Newport, in spite of the visits which Edith and Teddy paid and the increasing number of people who came to stay with them, Edith felt restless. Teddy, who never had too much to do, liked company and found the winters in Newport long. They added a fresh activity to their lives by taking a tiny house in New York on Madison Avenue, which Edith employed herself once more in arranging. By spending the worst of the winter there, they might manage to get through the rest of their lives in Newport.

It was in the little house, only sixteen feet wide over-all, that Edith worked off the excitement of the most thrilling moment of her life by tearing madly up and down the stairs, brandishing three letters from different magazines. She had sent them a poem each, and all had been accepted.

It must have been not long after her marriage that travel had once more stimulated verse. But Edith had not the habit of regular work. She wrote slowly and always polished with care. In spite of the little volume published in Newport, she hardly dared suppose that anybody would want to read what she wrote. Edith had grown up in a society where people did not write in a professional way. Her scribblings were reserved for private enjoyment. So ingrained was this view that later on when Edith became famous, none of her countless cousins, save one who was widely known as rather eccentric, ever spoke to her of her books. It may perhaps also be that Edith's critical mind unconsciously told her that her poetry was never going to be first-class. Intelligent, emotional, and containing fine passages or lines, it never succeeded in striking out a style of its own. In fact, if Edith's verses had been scattered among the minor poems of Robert Browning, Matthew Arnold, Tennyson, and Walt Whitman, they might have sunk into their surroundings without trace. Their real significance lay in their instant acceptance at a time when Edith was seriously struggling with prose.

Her deepest motive for turning to authorship may have lain in the failure of her marriage. She and Teddy had established a pleasant companionship, but little more. Edith had attempted to fill up the void by making a great many friends, chiefly men, who dined or stayed with her and Teddy to enjoy her conversation. She had drunk deep of European culture. She had employed the vacancy of her days by organizing perfection in one house after another. It was not enough. Essentially creative, she had no outlet which satisfied the deep things within her. The real Edith, so long denied and starved, so perfectly smothered by the empty good things of life, demanded attention.

The winters in New York may have represented a last effort to adapt her life to her inner needs. More and more Edith was learning to rely on the meeting of minds which takes place in good conversation. Unfortunately, the only society she knew well could not provide her with much companionship. Extravagance in New York had reached such a pitch that even the wealthy were bored with it. They sought new sensations in the only way they could think of. A man gave a dinner for his dog and presented him with a fifteen-thousand-dollar diamond collar. Cigarettes at another orgy were rolled in hundred-dollar bills. At yet another, each guest found a magnificent black pearl in his oysters. Costume balls had progressed to the point where a set of armor inlaid with gold was known to have cost ten thousand dollars. Most of Edith's friends had dropped out. Still exclusive and dining only with one another, they were a dispirited crowd, contemptuous of new values, but without much to offer. Real leadership of the social set had gone elsewhere. With it, all chance of being sought after by more interesting people than either the moneyed crowd or the old blue-bloods had vanished. The lack of interest taken by society in matters of culture may be illustrated by one of Edith's own anecdotes.

Some time after she herself had gained a reputation, Edith learned from one of her cousins that a certain New York party was to be a daring experiment. Literary persons, though socially unacceptable, had been invited. Times were changing, and a fashionable hostess had determined to lead the van. With a good deal of curiosity, Edith attended. She discovered that the literary guests were three: an old New York acquaintance who very occasionally contributed a column to a daily newspaper, the New York correspondent of the *Morning Post*, and herself. They were seated, so she says, "a little below the salt," thus making a social distinction between the best people and those who had marketed their talents. Edith laughed at the memory, but she was always quick to resent any sign of patronage. She must have been angry.

New York circles were depressing indeed for a vigorous woman in her early thirties, bursting with energy and overflowing with ideas. The few elderly and cultured dilettantes who were Edith's best friends in New York did not suffice her.

Edith was restless and dissatisfied. There is a story which might quite well be true that she went to Dr. Weir Mitchell, a Newport neighbor, to consult him about the frustrations of her marriage, which were preying on her health. Dr. Mitchell, a pioneer neurologist of the time, had also blossomed out in middle life as a popular novelist. He is said to have advised Edith to turn her energies to writing. Whether he did so or not, the fact is that she did begin in an unsystematic, occasional way to work at prose. In 1891, an unobtrusive little tale of New York life called "Mrs. Manstey's View" appeared in *Scribner's Magazine*. From that time on, perhaps once a year for some while, she would publish a short story. Edward Burlingame, the magazine's editor, eventually suggested that she put together a collection of her stories, which Scribners would publish.

Authors are temperamental, and those who deal with them need patience. Edith soon proved herself exceptionally trying. It was not that she quarreled with Burlingame. On the contrary, she was grateful for his understanding, inscribed him forthwith on the growing list of her friends, and put herself out to entertain him socially. But the full force of her personality was beginning to make itself felt. There was nothing restrained or cautious about Edith. Even the dearest of friends, Henry James, later referred to her as "the angel of devastation." It was an apt description, never more fitting than in her relations with the firm of Scribners.

Her immediate reaction was to overwhelm her editor with stories, some half finished, others mere ideas conceived quite possibly in his office in the midst of a conversation. He cautioned her gently not to let herself become a magazine bore. She took the criticism well, though the spate of her feelings rolled on unchecked. Suddenly, however, she would get ill or buzz off abroad, leaving plans in the air. Months later she would take up writing again, send in outlines of stories, want Burlingame's verdict by return mail or cable. She would promise to finish her collection by a definite date and would not do so. After writing three letters in one week and apparently tottering on the edge of completing a long-promised task, she would abandon it for a new idea, informing Burlingame that she would finish it better after a change. These postponements became a regular feature of all that she wrote. They were especially harassing to Scribners because the books that the firm published appeared first of all in their magazine. Books may be postponed; short stories can come out in later issues. Serials, however, can hardly be juggled back and forth at the author's convenience. The unhappy Burlingame was never really safe when he got an installment. Only too often Edith wanted it back at once for alterations. At the least she would cable, "Hold page 55 for important correction." Frequently when she made this sort of demand she was in Europe, three weeks away by mail in those days, and often more. Worse still her "type-writer," as she persisted in calling her favorite typist, remained in New York. Worse yet, no draft was ever final. Galley proof or page proof were merely challenges to make improvements. Edith was incapable of pronouncing any piece of writing finished.

Her enthusiasms were almost worse than her postponements. Edith had so many ideas and had to have all of them translated into action at once. After waiting very nearly six years to complete her first book of short stories, *The Greater Inclination*, she wanted it published within a few months to suit her convenience because she was going abroad. She had already her favorite printer, Daniel Updike of the Merrymount Press in Boston. Mr. Updike, an opinionated man, was hard to deal with from New York, but Edith insisted. Before the startled editors of Scribners had had time to look around, she had made arrangements with Macmillan for an English edition and was negotiating with reviewers in London to notice her book. Soon, she was talking with her Paris friends about a French translation. Meanwhile, she had made a study of the efforts of various publishers to advertise their wares and found the policy of Scribners unsatisfactory. She said so, handsomely admitting, "I don't of course flatter myself that there is any hope of modifying the business methods of the firm, but I think myself justified in protesting against them in my own case." A little later she is describing the cover of her book as "penitential" and suggesting an issue in white and gold for the holiday season. Surprisingly, her publishers gave in to this vagary and sent her a copy of the white-and-gold edition.

Hardly was a book in her hands before Edith was complaining about misprints. So invariable is this cry that it leads to the suspicion that she was trying to make yet further alterations. No detail was too small to attract her attention. In proof on one occasion she complained that the three dots used to indicate the breaking off of a sentence were too widely spaced. "You could drive a coach through them," she wrote in a fury. Two letters were needed to obtain a set of proofs with this corrected. In the new version, however, there were sometimes four dots instead of three. Fresh correspondence ensued, and all was finally well—though other alterations went on as a matter of course on every proof. The misplaced commas that Edith talked about whenever a book came out are very likely mere afterthoughts of her own. Nothing ever satisfied her.

Meanwhile, she was pressing to be paid. What about an advance? True, the contract which she signed made no mention of one; but she had supposed this was understood. She accepted the firm's explanation of its procedure, but she accepted also the advance which on this special occasion they agreed to give her. Using this as a precedent next time, she asked for and once more obtained a special advance. But her regular royalty payments? She never remembered when these were due and always blithely expected them very soon after the book came out. Disappointed, she wrote to inquire. After many years of this treatment, her publishers took a reproachful tone. She replied from Europe that of course she trusted them completely—indeed, so completely that she had spent the money on a picture before they had paid it.

The statement is revealing. Truth is, Edith did not need the money. For that very reason she saw no necessity to save it at all. It existed merely to make possible for her things she otherwise could not do. Thus when she saw something she wanted or got involved in something expensive, she dashed off a letter to Scribners and drove hard bargains. Since her activities were unceasing, this happened often.

In sum, one may say that Edith's relationship to her publishers was every bit as lively as to the rest of the world. To be sure, she did nothing peculiar. Other authors are also full of ideas, and some of them are harder to deal with. The trouble with Edith was the tempo of her mind. Either she rained a deluge of suggestions of all kinds, or else she was off somewhere, stirring up something else, and un-get-at-able.

Her volume of short stories developed slowly because she had not the habit of regular work and her other activities often absorbed her. Her health, moreover, was not robust. She suffered from hay fever and an unremitting series of colds and bronchial troubles. On one occasion she did not write to Burlingame for a year and broke the silence to explain she had been very ill. There is no suggestion that any of these complaints was directly connected with the frustrations of her marriage. She contented herself with observing that a climate which agreed with Teddy did not suit her, and vice versa. All the same, there is no doubt that she was not satisfied. Her growing awareness of the problem may be fitly illustrated by a story called "The Fullness of Life," which she published in 1893.

A woman died and after death met the Spirit of Life, who questioned her about her experience on earth.

" 'You did not find the fullness of life in your marriage?'

'Oh dear no,' she replied with an indulgent scorn. 'My marriage was a very incomplete affair.' "

She goes on to say that her inner life had been like a great house full of rooms, in the inmost of which she sat alone. Her husband had never got beyond the family living room of this house, where he thought they were both completely happy.

" 'His boots creaked,' " she says, " 'and he always slammed the door when he went out, and he never read

anything but railway novels and the sporting advertise-
ments in the papers—and—in short, we never understood each other in the least.' "

The most vivid emotional experience of her life had
taken place in a little church in Florence into which
they had come unexpectedly while a mass was going on.
She had felt herself mystically one with the beauty of
the ages. Her husband had sat beside her with his head
bowed decently, looking into the inside of his hat. Eventually he had remarked that there seemed little to see and
that dinner at their hotel was at six-thirty.

The Spirit of Life introduces the woman to her true
soul-mate, and they excitedly discover all they have in
common. But before they go off to spend eternity together, it occurs to the woman to ask if her husband
will also find his soul-mate in death. The spirit reminds
her that her husband was perfectly happy in his marriage. He will therefore look for her, and no other soul-
mate will suit him.

The woman begins to think of how helpless her husband is without her. Why, she even had to pick out his
mystery stories! She was fond of him in a way, and he
depended utterly on her. He would never understand
how it was that she had been dissatisfied. She could not
hurt him. She said goodbye to her soul-mate and that it
had been nice to meet him. Then she sat herself down
at the gate of heaven to wait for her husband.

One must not be too literal with a creative artist. We

may be certain that Teddy's boots never creaked and that when Edith had her mystic experience of beauty in a church, Teddy did not sit beside her peering into the crown of his hat. The wife's decision to stand by the man who needs her most may not precisely represent Edith's personal reasons for enduring her husband. All the same, we can hardly suppose that the subject of the story is not related to Edith's life. We may even wonder what Teddy thought when he first read it. Perhaps he never did read it. His attitude to Edith's writing was admiring, but he never understood it in the least. This was especially unfortunate because Edith really did need help from someone. She still lacked confidence and could not beyond a point take up Edward Burlingame's time. Besides, she was not always in New York. She required, or thought she did, a literary adviser. Presently she found one.

When a drawer in Edith's desk was beginning to get cluttered with stories and poems in various stages, Ogden Codman and she finally decided to write a book called *The Decoration of Houses* which was intended to show that the proper purpose of interior decoration is to bring out the proportions of a well-designed room, not to smother it with lace and fringe and velvet. The whole subject was a new one for a popular book, and there were a great many ideas on their minds. Edith plunged into the text.

She did not find her task easy. The subject reduced

itself to a scattered list of details. Without experience in organizing her thoughts, without training in writing school themes or college papers, Edith had no idea how to weld a mass together or to interest her public. She wrote a great deal and was clever enough to see it would not do. She began to despair.

She showed her manuscript at last to Walter Berry, the distant cousin who had fascinated her years ago and then gone out of her life. Walter Berry, a rising Washington lawyer by now, was a voracious reader and a man of wide knowledge in literary and artistic fields. More of a critic than an original mind, he had the experience which Edith happened to lack. He glanced through the pages of *The Decoration of Houses* and burst into laughter. When he recovered, however, he had the patience to spend weeks with Edith going through the manuscript, illustrating the principles of organization and pruning her style. She drank in the lesson. Edith's instincts and the whole bent of her mind fitted her for what he was saying. Walter Berry was guiding her onto the track which was really hers.

The Decoration of Houses was one of those experiments in a new field which publishers are afraid to undertake. It hung fire for some years, while in the meantime, Edith was producing her collection of short stories. She had no fixed routines and frequently no time. She did, however, continue to consult Walter Berry, who was by now established as her literary adviser. In the circumstances, he did his best not to interfere with her growing talent. Chiefly his comments concerned construction and style, leaving Edith to choose and develop her own themes. However, in her gratitude she deferred more and more to his opinion, so that the influence of Walter Berry began to cast a long shadow across her life. Inevitably, as the years went by, Teddy dwindled. His little Pussy might be fond of him still, but the talented writer who was emerging into the full light of day led her own life in complete independence. Inside it, she was forming connections from which Teddy must be shut out. Neither Edward Burlingame nor Walter Berry worked with the girl whom Teddy Wharton thought he had married.

Chapter 4

SUCCESS AND SORROW

IN 1897, after prolonged crises such as only Edith knew how to raise over illustrations, *The Decoration of Houses* finally appeared. Edith's first volume of stories, entitled *The Greater Inclination* came out two years later. The latter event provides a vivid illustration of the two souls which dwelt in her. Looking back on the occasion from the misty heights of old age, it was not the English edition, the white-and-gold cover, the lack of enterprise in Scribners' advertising which had impressed her. She had forgotten her strenuous efforts to run the publishing business. What she recollected was her astounded naïveté. Two books published, one of them the fruit of her imagination! And the critics were actually kind! She could hardly believe it. Yet on her regular travels that year as she passed through London, she went into a bookstore to buy something to read. The salesman actually pressed on her *The Greater Inclination* as the latest London hit.

Unreal, impossible though it might seem, she was a success.

This was probably not a surprise to Edith Wharton, however startled Edith Jones may have felt. She had been bombarding her publishers for figures of sales when the book was only a few weeks off the presses. Yet it is one thing to know, another to comprehend. She was really bewildered, though the success of *The Greater Inclination* was actually modest. Edith had pleased her public without sweeping it off its feet. Indeed, as we look back at *The Greater Inclination*, over a gap of nearly seventy years, it may seem difficult to understand why the book attracted notice. These are not stories of violent action, nor do they deal with their subjects in a sensational way. Edith Wharton's half-dozen best stories are extraordinarily good; but none of these appeared in *The Greater Inclination*, or even in *Crucial Instances* two years later. What was it that for a moment or two set London talking?

In the first place one may say that the tales were really well written, and in a style which was fresher then than it seems now. They are in fact very far superior to "Mrs. Manstey's View" or "The Fullness of Life." The painstaking six years which had gone to produce this little volume were not all wasted time. Edith had profited from Walter Berry's instructions and Burlingame's advice. Her friends had taught her restraint, but they had managed not to destroy her self-confidence in the process. The result was a style both clear and sharp—too sharp, some said. Minor characters or scenes in a short story need to be sketched in outline. Edith soon proved herself particularly skillful at tossing off people in a quick, contemptuous phrase. "The bishop always entered a room well." We know immediately that we are not intended to like this particular bishop. "One of those searching American days so calculated to reveal the shortcomings of our street-cleaning and the excesses of our architecture." The author's contempt for the American city of her day needs no elaboration. This kind of cleverness has a bitter flavor piquant in late Victorian days when the reading public was tired of gluey sentiments and improving morals. Edith's plots were unsentimental too. A man who has once shown cowardice spends his life looking vainly for a second chance. He feels a failure, never perceiving that his steadfastness in resisting a nagging wife shows daily courage. A woman, supposed the mistress of a famous dead writer, wrestles with the inner knowledge that she was only his intellectual companion while he looked elsewhere for love. In sum, Edith's viewpoint was a little new—never shocking or completely repelling her public, but not giving precisely what it expected.

Her work was thought-provoking as well. Almost all Edith's plots discuss a moral problem from an intelligent standpoint. Many of them deal with the special concerns of artists and writers, revealing the author's bent and breadth of culture. What was more, she writes freely about problems of marriage. Her longest story in *The Greater Inclination* is "Souls Belated," which tells how Lydia, who has run away with Gannet, refuses to marry him when she gets her divorce. Her argument is that they have both agreed that conventional marriage is an unworthy thing. Since they have already had the courage to defy convention, Lydia refuses to submit to it again. Unfortunately, life soon shows her that she is weaker than she thinks, cares more for social approval, and is not capable of the grand gesture. She will marry Gannet, and one rather wonders whether they will be happy.

A story of this kind is worth outlining because conventional marriage and its problems lay at the bottom of Edith's life. It is also fair to point out that the tone she takes about it is not particularly common for female writers in 1899. She is not eager to defend it. Lydia's elopement is not regarded as wrong. Even though Gannet quite steadily tries to make her an honest woman, she remains unquestionably the finer spirit. She bruises herself against the facts of life and is damaged. We pity her and see her error, but we do not condemn her. It seems not unlikely that what attracted the public to Edith's work at first was "Souls Belated."

At all events, *The Greater Inclination* was a success, and Edith's courage mounted. She soon had need of it all because she had plunged not only into her first novel, but into a work for which all her knowledge of Italian culture, detailed though it now was, must be insufficient. *The Valley of Decision*, which was finally published in 1902, is a long historical novel about eighteenth-century Italy. It is impressive for the quality of its descriptions, the extraordinary amount of learning which it reveals, and the amazing way in which it manages to make the period come to life. Unhappily, however, it makes tedious reading. All the characters are carefully typical of the period or the cause they represent. The result is that the major characters never come to life at all, while the minor ones are apt to get lost in the background. It is the background which everybody praises, and with justice. But background does not make a book, especially a long one. As a work of art, *The Valley of Decision* falls dead. In her book of memoirs written not long before her death, Edith claims that its immense erudition was not a product of research, but of the knowledge that she had soaked in during travel and by reading for pleasure. The statement is incredible and not literally true. It is the case, however, that an accurate memory and a persistent attention to detail had really given her an unusual breadth of knowledge. No estimate of Edith can be complete without appreciating the culture which made possible such a work without many years of special preparation.

The Valley of Decision was received if not with enthusiasm, at least with respect. Short stories and novelettes were also appearing in regular sequence. So far Edith had not tried her hand at a serious novel which could claim to be more than a vivid re-creation of background. She was both afraid of and attracted by the prospect. The little social world of New York had emerged as her proper field, yet how could anything of real significance be made out of the life led either by her parents or by the millionaire parvenus who had replaced them? Edith said to herself that a trivial society must gain significance from the life which it destroys. Deliberately she set out to create such a life, and she produced Lily Bart.

Lily Bart, the heroine of *The House of Mirth,* became a creature over whom a whole generation wept. Incidentally, she raised her creator into the front rank of American novelists and rewarded her with considerable sums of pocket money. Lily was a beautiful, frivolous, expensive girl, formed for soft living, educated by an ambitious mother, but left badly off. In order to live the only life possible for her, Lily must make herself useful to wealthier women and she must marry money. Unluckily, her instincts are too refined for the life that she is leading. She balks at capturing a dull rich man and lets herself be seen with Lawrence Selden, an attractive bachelor without enough money to support two people in comfort. The pair discuss how to rise above their surroundings, a luxury which Selden on his bachelor's income can just afford. Poor Lily, slightly compromised

by her imprudent intimacy, is forced to make conces-
sions to the convenience of her hostesses which tend to
involve further degradation. Gradually she descends in
the social scale, always too much of a lady to seize a
chance for success in an unscrupulous world. The end
is an overdose of sleeping pills for Lily, while Selden,
who has almost made up his mind to marry her, comes
only in time to drop a kiss on her lifeless corpse. The
sentimentality of the conclusion is redeemed by Edith's
merciless scorn, which embraces the material standards
of society, the ineffectiveness of Selden, the futility of
Lily's own aims, and the drab alternative of living in a
single room on her pitiful income. *The House of Mirth*
is a powerful novel written about social values which do
not in themselves appear worthwhile. In 1905, it had a
more forcible impact because the group Edith wrote
about still existed and was still interesting to America at
large. Fashions change. *The House of Mirth* is dated,
and for that reason out of style. It is not, however, a bad
novel which happened to hit the taste of its day. It is a
good novel which does not happen to hit ours. Like so
many of Edith's better works, it is worth reading.

The success of *The House of Mirth* made Edith's
reputation and for the time being, the fortune of Scribners. Never had the firm known a work which had sold
so widely so fast. Edith received fan mail with the most
extraordinary raptures. One excited reader rushed out to
send a wire, "Lily Bart is dead!" when the story ended.

A prominent playwright was soon persuaded to undertake a stage version which opened in Albany by way of a tryout. It was not successful there, and Edith insisted that the third act be rewritten. One of the reporters present at the opening reported a quarrel between the co-authors, including fragments of repartee which Edith indignantly denied. There is, however, no doubt that she made herself a nuisance with her usual bright ideas and passion for improvements. In spite of its bad start, the play went on to New York; but it had a very short run. Golden visions dissolved. Edith had to put up for the moment with her considerable royalties from the novel.

The House of Mirth had found its authoress an amateur. It left her a professional. Edith had addressed herself to the creation of Lily Bart in her usual spasmodic way, but had been faced by an unexpected demand from Scribners. The magazine was serializing *The House of Mirth* before publication, and the dates were all arranged when another author unexpectedly let Burlingame down. Edith, who was always optimistic at the start, had written glowingly about her progress. Burlingame appealed to her to deliver her work six months ahead of schedule. Knowing what he already did about Edith's habits, this was rash in the extreme. Undoubtedly the experience aged him. Edith, though taken aback, could not well refuse. At last she was forced to organize her activities around a regular time for writing. With every maddening postponement and last-minute change,

Burlingame did get his installments. Edith had by no means revolutionized her methods of work, but she had learned the discipline of continuous effort. Like the lessons of Walter Berry, this sunk in deeply. Edith's new position as a leading American authoress found her ready to apply herself seriously. The transition suited her nature, and yet it was no trifling one. Nobody in her father's house or her own had hitherto buckled down to steady work. By doing so, Edith was building a bridge to a world far different from the amateur one she was used to. To be sure, she still lived on the amateur side; but new vistas opened.

Her first real intimacy with an important writer had begun in 1893. Paul Bourget is not one of the giants of French literature, yet he won his place in the Académie Française. In his day he counted for something. His reputation, though shrunken somewhat with time, has not departed. The man, moreover, was greater than his works. He was, to be sure, a stout reactionary and something of a snob, preferring the rarified atmosphere of an aristocratic *salon* to the liberal, freethinking, or materialist tone of the Third French Republic. With all this, however, he was a man of wide culture and fascinating conversation. He had taken the trouble to travel slowly and at leisure with the object of broadening his mind. Pursuing this policy, he came to America in 1893 and having a commission to write about a fashionable watering place, he appeared in Newport. With Edith's international connections it was only natural that he should meet her.

Meeting people for the first time was an experience throughout the whole of Edith's life which was fraught with peril. She was always shy with strangers and afraid of well-known people. Greatly wishing to impress, she was apt to call up her aristocratic manners and offend, precisely when she tried to be pleasing. Yet equally often, a joke shared or a gesture would sweep her reserve away, so that her fascination became apparent. When that happened, she had made a friend for life. It seems to have happened at once with Paul Bourget. We do not know the details, but a tale from some years later may serve to illustrate Edith's two manners of meeting intelligent people.

She first met Bernard Berenson, the famous expert on Italian art, at a tea party in Florence. Berenson was a great name in his field, and Edith was shy. She assumed her party manner; and Berenson, who was used to a good deal of deference from strangers, found her offensively rude. She sneered, he said. She jeered. She turned up her nose at every subject. In short, she was an impossible woman; and he made up his mind that he would not meet her again. Some months later he visited Paris, where he had many friends, and discovered that Edith and Teddy were wintering there too. Thereupon he refused every invitation unless he was assured that he would not meet Mrs. Wharton. This became exceed-

ingly awkward. They moved in the same circles, and
their friends could not put up with the situation. Accordingly, Berenson was inveigled to a party which was
held in the dimmest of light—he said merely by fire-
light. He was led up by his host to a lady in a corner
whose name he did not catch. He sat down politely and
plunged into conversation. What a marvelous woman!
They shared the same enthusiasms, capped each other's
jokes, and conversed with more fire and spirit than he
could ever remember. He found himself in contact with
a rare personality. In half an hour he had made an intimate friend. And presently, when the lights were fully
turned up, he saw it was Edith. Naturally in the course
of their later acquaintance, he teased her about her manner when they had first met. She had been completely
unconscious of giving offense. All she could remember
was how frightened she had felt.

Luckily for Bourget, and for Edith as well, their
meeting in 1893 was one of the occasions when Edith
forgot to be shy. And once such a connection was made,
she was indefatigable in pursuing it. She soon became as
fond of Minnie Bourget as of Paul, visited them, entertained them in Paris or London, took them with her on
her travels, and gained even more than she gave. The
Bourgets knew everyone in the international group
which considered Paris the center of culture. This world
was now open for Edith to step into; and gradually as
her reputation increased, her courage mounted.

The ugly house at Newport had not lasted the Whartons long, in spite of the alterations of Ogden Codman. Edith was really tired of Newport. Her bronchial troubles were always at their worst in the Newport climate. Teddy, though he liked the place more than she, was fond of the Berkshires which he had known as a child. His father had died, as had her mother; and their combined fortunes had been increased by inheritance. Edith's earnings, in addition, were comfortably large. In short, they could now afford a big country place where Teddy could oversee the out-of-doors and do all the riding he wanted. Edith, whose attitude towards a horse was cautious, did not care much for her husband's pursuits. She was happy, however, to create another garden, to fill the place with guests, and to explore the countryside with them. She and Teddy took a house at Lenox for the summer and plunged into the fascinating business of building their dream house.

"The Mount," though no particular architectural gem, was large and spacious. It was in fact enormous in modern terms, containing a library, drawing room, and dining room, this last opening onto a terrace overlooking a formal garden and shaded from the sun by a vast canvas awning. Below the garden were lawns and meadows stretching to a little lake. Like her mother's, Edith's drawing rooms were painfully tidy. Almost too much trouble had been taken to see that every object pleased the eye. Yet there were piles of books around, and in the guest rooms every imaginable comfort was provided. Guests who were writers like herself found a well-stocked desk with every writing convenience and free time till eleven o'clock in the morning. Edith by then had put her own writing aside and was ready for the day. She was not, as far as her neighbors were concerned, particularly social. She thought the summer crowd dull and did not scruple to express her opinion rather freely. What she liked to do was to plan little excursions through the countryside with her own guests. In earlier years these had been made by carriage; but in 1902 she had been commissioned to write the text of an illustrated volume on Italian villas and their gardens. This very naturally had involved a good deal of driving around Italy to inspect villas. In the course of this she was invited by the American ambassador at the time to make one excursion, a round trip of some fifty miles, with him in his new motor.

The motor car was a revelation to Edith. Its speed and convenience charmed her utterly. True, this was before the days of the windshield; and not only was she blown about, but she was speechless for several days with laryngitis. This did not deter her. She knew a good thing when she saw one and never rested till she had a car of her own in which she was driven through the heat of an Italian summer wearing a hood with a mica mask through which she peered out at the landscape. When the windshield appeared, her bliss was complete.

Even the unreliability of the early automobile was less of a trouble to her than to most, since her chauffeur changed tires or fussed with the engine. Occasional breakdowns, accepted as a matter of course, were still far less tiresome than always being confined to train or carriage. Why, from Lenox it was possible now in a single day to visit the Nortons some thirty miles off!

Thus Edith and Teddy filled their days at "The Mount." By building a home of their own they had really intended to settle down. Their life together was amicable enough, since they had a good many superficial things in common. Teddy made a pleasant host and could be amusing. He and Edith shared a certain fastidiousness, though occasionally Edith would even put up with bad breeding from interesting people. Both were quick to despise pushing inferiors, yet they never put on airs with their own dependents. Their servants' convenience was always carefully considered. In local visits, they took special pains to be agreeable to a governess whom they thought badly treated. In other words, the pair got on easily; and where their interests differed, they went their own ways. She had her little lap dogs, he his outdoor ones. She had her publishers and literary friends, he his salmon fishing with his brother and old cronies up in New Brunswick. She had her garden planning; he managed the estate. If she found him unsympathetic to her real interests, she could fill the house with other people or retire to her creative work. And if he did not un-

derstand her mind, he was at least proud to indulge her
and to see her qualities valued.

It was a well-planned life, but the seeds of its destruc-
tion were in it from the beginning. Early in their first
real summer at "The Mount," Teddy caught the grippe.
He was a bad patient, and grippe is depressing. Teddy's
symptoms soon became those of complete nervous
breakdown. Worse still, they were irrational. Unable
to make up his mind on the merest trifles, he would leap
suddenly to strange conclusions, either about his symptoms, which obsessed him, or about the ways in which
he was being treated. Fits of unreasoning anger followed, or else he retreated into some world of his own
which had no connection with the facts of daily life.
The doctors agreed that he was out of his mind, but insisted that his state was due to the grippe and not uncommon. They spoke hopefully of his recovering when
he grew physically stronger. Their encouragement was
all very well, but the facts were ominous. Teddy's father had been a mental patient at the time of Edith's
marriage, and the doctors had assured her then that the
complaint was not inheritable. Now they talked of
grippe and of recovery; but Teddy was ill for three
grim months, and the experience was shattering. Neither
of them could be quite certain thereafter that it would
not be repeated. The doctors merely suggested taking
life easily.

It must have taxed Edith's ingenuity to think of a

manner in which Teddy could lead an easier life than he was used to. No doubt to be so constantly outshone by his wife was a great strain, just as his lack of understanding was hard on Edith. But this situation was rooted in the nature of both. No compromise could have dimmed Edith's personality. No effort of Teddy's could make him comprehend. He looked, she tells us, on her writing simply as witchcraft. It almost frightened him as something uncanny.

Teddy's situation called for inexhaustible patience and loving watchfulness. They were not Edith's strong points. In minor matters, she was never a woman who put up with much. She was used to making demands in daily living. Consuelo Vanderbilt spoke of Teddy trailing after Edith picking up her feather boa, more like an equerry than a husband. Edith herself said that on one Italian trip which they took by coach with the Bourgets, Teddy went ahead on a bicycle every day to arrange their accommodations. Very likely the horse-drawn coach was too slow and the intellectual conversation bored him. Teddy's situation all the same seems most unusual for a husband. Yet within the limits of her nature and upbringing, Edith did consider Teddy. She really did make him an object of tender concern. Undoubtedly the most important thing in their lives was to avoid a recurrence by caring for Teddy's physical health. It became understood that Teddy was not strong and winters in Lenox were not to be thought of. They

had retained a little house in New York. Perhaps that
would do.

Unfortunately, it did not. Neither of them liked the
climate of New York, while the general atmosphere of
the place did not suit Edith. Within a year or two she
was known as a novelist of international repute but
slender output. Friends told Teddy that she ought to
develop her talent. There are people who have written
immortal works in retirement, but temperaments and
subjects differ. Those who, like Edith, write about the
social scene, need to mix with others and study the
world. Indeed this was particularly so in her case, since
her whole being was stimulated by the cut-and-thrust
of exchanging ideas. Unhappily, New York did not provide this. The real cut-and-thrust of the sprawling city
was commercial, and its most vigorous literary life was
journalistic. Such society as Edith might have wanted
to mix with met at the Century Club and included no
women. Her own circle was as dull and limited as ever.
Her literary eminence was a positive drawback there.

Too quiet a life did not suit Teddy either, that is, not
for the whole year. He really seems to have loved "The
Mount," yet he and Edith were constantly turning
to travel, even during parts of the summer. In 1904,
the very year after Teddy's breakdown, Edith discovered an Italian watering place, Salso Maggiore,
which wrought a miracle on her own health. She went
regularly thereafter, sometimes twice in a summer; and
her bronchial troubles seemed to fade away. But with

the best will in the world, one cannot visit an Italian spa and spend all summer at Lenox. Edith got in the habit of sailing alone, leaving Teddy behind to enjoy the fishing or shooting and to follow after. Then part of the spring and fall or part of the winter would be spent in Europe. One or other of the Whartons always seemed to be crossing the ocean. The enormous place at Lenox, in spite of all its amenities, saw less and less of them. Possibly one problem was that the intimacy of life in the country did expose Teddy too closely to Edith's overpowering personality. Fill "The Mount" with guests as they would, there must have been many and many a time of tête à tête which perhaps was not welcome. And if Teddy's spirits appeared distressed, it was natural to try and divert him with travel. Teddy's spirits loomed terribly in both their lives; a year or so later he had a second, though a shorter breakdown.

For all these reasons, "The Mount" failed of its purpose. Its graciousness, its wealth, and its comfort were symbols of the life that the Whartons apparently had. Beneath them lay restlessness and tension. Edith had come into her own as a writer, and everything seemed to be going her way. But she was not by any means detached enough to view the prospects of Teddy's health without dismay. She was truly fond of him, and he still adored her. Very often she must have been at her wit's end. Eventually nothing was to stay the steady march of his degeneration.

Chapter 5

THE JAMESIAN CIRCLE

By FAR the most important American literary figure of the nineties was Henry James, twenty years older than Edith, but of a quite similar background. His father, usually called Henry James the Elder to distinguish him from Henry himself, had been a man of means. Unlike George Frederic Jones, however, Henry the Elder was a man of strong intellectual tastes who became a philosopher and theologian of some note. In other words, the atmosphere in Henry James's home had been far more intelligent and purposeful than that of Edith's. It was at least equally cosmopolitan. For seven years during adolescence Henry was educated in England, France, Switzerland, and Germany. In 1862 he entered the Harvard Law School, not being physically strong enough for the Civil War. At Harvard, he attracted the attention of William Dean Howells and of Charles Eliot Norton, who was to become Edith's great friend. They encouraged him to write, and from his early twenties he devoted himself to the pursuit of literature.

He did it in his own way, which was not like anybody else's. It is a common view that direct experience is essential for a great writer. He must get around, go through his own tragedies, have his own adventures, learn greatness by actual doing. He must become aware of life in every aspect—political, social, mystical, personal, physical, even unconscious. For only what a man has made his own can he express. This is all very true, no doubt; yet like most sweeping views, it is only true in a way. Direct experience appeared to Henry James a mere distraction from what he wanted to do. He never married, never sought adventure, took no interest in political or social problems, left speculations about the meaning of life to his brother William, the famous philosopher. Henry James concentrated with narrow tenacity on personal relations between people who were cultured enough to be subtle, wealthy enough to be freed from economic pressures, and cosmopolitan enough to be complex. He had early decided that the group he wished to portray was centered in Europe, and from 1876 he lived permanently in England. His chief experience of life came through conversation. Hermit-like in his devotion to his art, James was at the same time intensely social. French he spoke with absolute perfection. London for many years was his home. His family connections, his independent means, his

growing reputation made him a welcome guest for
many a hostess on either side of the Channel. He alter-
nated his social periods with strict retirement; and he
finally settled in 1898 at the charming little English sea-
port town of Rye, remote enough for privacy, yet near
to London for easy visits.

James's reputation had been made in 1879 with *Daisy
Miller*, which had been a best seller. He had never been
read widely since, though *Portrait of a Lady*, which
many consider his masterpiece, had been moderately
successful. In fact, his literary stature had grown while
his sales did not. James never understood the reason for
this. He would have liked the popularity enjoyed by
Thomas Hardy, Meredith, Conrad, and other writers
of his day; and he felt he deserved it. In fact, he hardly
did. Detailed, infinitely subtle, a little bloodless, the
lovely features of James's heroines smile at us through
a multitude of fine-drawn lines which challenge us to
admire their portraits as technique. But the public fancy
will always be for something bolder, more highly col-
ored. Admiration James must command, but those who
love him will be a select group.

This was true in his private life as well as his novels.
James was deeply affectionate, but the inner circle of
his friends was not large. His settling on the other side
of the Atlantic from his family had cut off his roots.
James was fifty in 1893; and his bachelor existence had
confirmed him in old-maidish habits, mannerisms, little

anxieties about his health, a barrage of little inquiries for keeping visitors at bay. He abounded, for instance, in compliments to ladies. American tourists were flatteringly induced to describe to him every detail of their trip. Visiting cousins were questioned by the hour about other cousins. "And you see, my dear," he would confide when the guests had departed, "they hadn't time to talk to me about my books."

James had, to be sure, his devoted intimates; but the social experience of a lifetime had made him particular about their choice. They had to be witty, intelligent, responsive, and were usually men. His single-minded attachment to his one object in life made it essential that his friends be literary in taste. Yet though he respected artists of his own caliber, he went his way and they theirs. James did not love flatterers, but he did need people around him who genuinely respected his work. His peculiar style, his conviction of its value, and his lack of popularity with the public all demanded a certain reassurance. In fact, James asked a good deal of his friends; but he gave generously in return. His confidences to them were unreserved. His humor, his unfailing kindness, the riches of his stored mind made his friendship a precious possession. There was, too, a quality of greatness about the man which his little oddities never for a moment obscured. There was no pretentiousness about him at all. He simply was himself, a man rare and unusual.

Into the select Jamesian group with its hesitations, delicacies, and odd little ways now strode Edith Wharton. She was brilliant, sure of herself, and had all the popular appeal that James aspired to. She was far more wealthy than he, more social, less single-minded—and a woman. She was twenty years younger, untiring, demanding, independent, clear-cut. She could not even read James's later books with pleasure, while he from his exalted heights looked down on hers. Edith swept in and one might almost say, added Henry James to her formidable collection of notable men. Yet the sensitive, elderly man over whose fixed habits she ruthlessly trampled loved her in an intimate friendship which was never clouded by jealousy of her success and never affected by the difference in her sex. Edith for her part treated James with respect as well as love, not forgetting that he was more distinguished than she and of greater talent.

Their acquaintance began in a manner typical of Edith—with a couple of false starts. Not long after her marriage, Edith and Teddy were invited to dine in company with Henry James in Paris. In great excitement, Edith put on her prettiest dress—a tea-rose pink embroidered with iridescent beads—in hopes of charming the great man. She failed to do so and was too shy to speak. A year or two later in Paris she relied on a lovely new hat, thinking that a compliment might give her the courage to blurt out her admiration. Edith had not yet found herself, and a good many years were to pass before her growing reputation and acquaintance with the same social circles in Europe brought the two together. In 1902, Minnie Cadwalader Jones, Freddy's wife, sent to James, Edith's early collections of short stories. In return he commented on her "diabolical little cleverness, the quality of intention and intelligence in her style, and her sharp eye for an interesting kind of subject. You have made me," he added, "want to get hold of the little lady and pump the pure essence of my wisdom and experience into her." In other words, he was condescending; but his attention and his kindness had been aroused. Nothing was ever a surer passport to James's favor than even the mildest sort of literary promise. Edith by now had grown up, so that they were ready to meet on common ground. When they did so, "It seemed," she said, "as if we had been always friends." In fact, they discovered an identical ironic sense of humor. In the course of an evening, it would be Edith's eye that James would seek with a gleam in his own, only to discover her quickness even greater than his, her glance as acute. Theirs became the unspoken intimacy of two natures that happened to fit. In addition, they delighted in each other's conversation.

Alike in humor, they were utterly different in style. James had conquered an early stammer which had left him with a maddening hesitation in speech. He was also constitutionally incapable of calling a spade a spade, not out of pomposity, but because the plain word did not express an exact shade of meaning. He would fumble for precisely what he did mean, stray away from it, come back, move around, survey without touching it. Eventually by a series of deft strokes he had created not a mere spade, but an artist's drawing of what the spade had meant to his mind at that moment. To some types of auditor it was a fatal temptation to prompt him with the word "spade" for which he appeared to be looking. To others, it was equally fatal to say the word impatiently in the head and not to listen while the artist very slowly sketched his subject. Edith, quick-witted, clear-headed though she was, could hear him out. Her social training, no doubt, had taught her this much. Then too, he was older and far more famous than she. At all events, she listened, found it rewarding, and mastered the technique. When he had made his point, she answered with complete comprehension. James's eye would gleam in reply, and there was nothing imperceptive or dull about the hesitations with which he addressed himself to further expansion.

Their intimacy ripened fast. In 1902 he had not met her—as far at least as he remembered. In 1904–5 he came to America, visited the Whartons in New York, and stayed at Lenox. A minor attraction which Edith had for him became evident now. James liked his comforts and a touch of luxury. As one of his old-maidish ways and as part quite possibly of his grudge against a public which did not read him, James had convinced himself that he was poor. In actuality, he lived in a charming house in Rye with devoted servants, a secretary, and had anything in reason required for the kind of life he chose to live. He imagined himself, however, as living like a Spartan. It gave him a feeling of fine superiority to revel in what he called Edith's "corrupting and succulent" meals, reminding himself that he was used to plainer fare. When she returned the visit, he was terribly torn between his natural kindness and his desire to score off her morally. In fact, he divided his time between hoping she was comfortable and expecting with pride and relish that she wasn't. In the atmosphere of "The Mount," where Edith's imagination anticipated every possible need, James had the satisfaction of enjoying himself while feeling superior to the mere comforts by which he was surrounded. To cap the climax, Edith possessed what to him was the supreme luxury of all, an automobile. Both he and she were devoted to motoring. They liked the motion. It gave a chance to explore the countryside. It brought friends nearer. It offered a splendid place for long conversations. Machines being what they then were, it even supplied a sense of adventure. Walter Berry, always welcome at "The Mount," records in italics a run of *sixty miles!* On another occasion Berry, Edith, and James were marooned by the roadside till the early hours of the morning while the chauffeur wrestled in vain with their engine. Even more delightful was the fact that motoring was breezy when a heat wave struck Lenox.

James felt the heat. He was by now in his sixties and had put on a great deal of weight. His big head, with its fine, impressive profile like a Roman emperor's on a coin, had become distinctly fleshy; and though he angrily ignored the fact, he had a paunch. Every inch of this generous expanse ran with perspiration when the temperature soared. Used to fussing over himself for want of anyone else to fuss about, he gave in groaning and staged a complete collapse. In vain Edith provided oranges for him to suck and disposed an electric fan to play on his person. Nothing rescued him from a state of utter despair but the sensation of driving through the Berkshire hills with the windows open. Finally Edith was inspired to suggest that he cut his visit short and advance his sailing date. He would be cooler when he got out onto the ocean. No proposal could have gone more utterly astray. To change long-term arrangements, get his laundry back, rescue some luggage which he had left with his brother, telegraph, catch unexpected trains, launch himself across the ocean spiritually unprepared for the change! He had always realized that Edith was a fearful and wonderful woman, but this! He could not understand her utter frivolity.

Thus Henry James moaned and groaned until he went on his way at the prearranged time. Edith might so easily have found him a nuisance. However, the charm of his company was really so great, his wit and wisdom and kindness so immense that his little foibles, absurd though they undoubtedly were, cast not the slightest cloud on their affection.

The situation was reversed when she visited him. It was now her turn to be demanding. In a way, Henry James invited this; for he felt that Edith should not center her European trips in Paris, as she now tended to do. She and Teddy had begun to travel increasingly in winter for the sake of Teddy's health and of his nerves. The New York house was in time given up, and they formed a habit of taking a flat in Paris, where the Bourgets were the center of a congenial social group. Henry James pressed London on them, but unhappily Teddy took a strong dislike to England. English society was divided into compartments, so that people who liked Edith merely despised the sporting set congenial to Teddy. He was often touchy now, and Edith's time in England became limited by his capacity to bear it. As a result, when she did arrive, she wanted everything dovetailed to suit her convenience. James was living quietly at Rye with his fixed hours, his cautious entertaining of one guest at a time, his inability to give instructions in simple words or make arrangements without fussing. All Edith's brilliant ideas and last-minute changes of plan were terrible to him. Long before she had so much as embarked in New York, he was really wringing his hands, either completely off schedule or

aware that he would become so when the Whartons arrived. His friends, though genuinely dazzled by Edith's
brilliance, her wealth, her maid, her chauffeur, her expensive turn-out, saw and resented for James the great
disturbance which her visits produced. Yet when Edith
arrived, she and he fell eagerly into each other's arms.
They worked every morning and used the rare treat of
Edith's automobile to explore the countryside. Nor did
the burden of entertainment fall on James for long. One
of his chief friends was Howard Sturgis, member of a
wealthy Boston clan, but educated and long ago settled
in England. Howard Sturgis, a bachelor like James,
lived comfortably at Windsor, complete with his own
family servants, old-maidish ways, fixed habits, and literary pursuits. He lived, however, in considerable comfort and liked to entertain a select group. His house, in
fact, was even more of a center for the little circle of
friends than James's own. Edith would readily transfer
her residence to Windsor, James coming with her. The
arrangement freed him from responsibility and fuss
while still allowing him to enjoy both Edith and her
motoring parties. For Sturgis himself, Edith felt an affection only second to that which she felt for James. She
pressed his new novel impulsively on Scribners, never
ceasing thereafter to lament her lack of success and the
discouragement of the author.

Her automobile remained a great attraction. In 1907,
she persuaded James to join her and Teddy in a motor

trip through France. Touring for pleasure and away from the railroad tracks was still an experience confined to very few. Despite intimate knowledge of France, neither James nor Edith was familiar with a stretch of the countryside which any tourist can easily drive through now. It was a highlight of their acquaintance. Teddy's health seems to have been good. No flaws of any kind developed, save the daily explosions which were a necessary part of travel with Edith.

The trouble was her standards were too high. Edith was always prepared to pay for the best, though she despised the senseless throwing of money around by rich Americans to whom expense meant nothing. But if she paid well, she also expected much. She was perfectly ready to have a whole new dinner specially cooked or to turn every arrangement in a hotel upside down to suit her convenience. Ceaselessly anxious for the comfort of her friends, she made as much fuss on their behalf as on her own. Occasionally, one of them, highly tried, would gently protest. "If the poor man were as intelligent as he would have to be to please you, he wouldn't be a waiter in this inn, but President of the French Republic." For the most part, they were forced to accept her little ways as a minor drawback compared to the stimulus of travel with a person so intensely alive and so aware of beauty in art, architecture, or scene.

She could write well about travel too. Her works on Italy, on her trip through France and later on, through

Morocco are full of vitality. They are fascinating still to those who like to explore through the pages of a book. She was doing her best work in those crowded years between the publication of *The House of Mirth* and the outbreak of the First World War. Words streamed from her pen: short stories, descriptions of travel, novelettes, two full-length novels, a volume of verse. There was a moment when she stood unchallenged at the top of the tree. American literature was in a transition stage and lacked great names. Henry James with his international milieu hardly counted as purely American by now. Edith, still rooted in New York, understood a small section of American life very well. Her critical attitude towards it was thought-provoking. Her reputation was considerable abroad, where American authors were by no means widely read. In fact, the critics were universally kind to Edith, and with reason. She was reaching the top of her powers.

This was far from the case with Henry James. He was approaching seventy by now, and his best creative work was all behind him. Indeed, since 1906, his major task had been the preparation of a complete edition of his works, which had involved him in a host of critical essays. In other words, he had not been making money. His expenses were really worrying him. He certainly was not on the verge of starvation, but he was too old to change his habits and too dependent on servants who had been with him half a lifetime. His conviction of his poverty was deepened as he perceived that the recognition for which he had so long yearned would always elude him. It was painful to contemplate the dazzling success of Edith, whose productions he did not greatly value. James's nature was above petty jealousy; but his honest conviction, shared by Edith and all his friends, was that his talent stood head and shoulders above hers. It was unfortunate that comparisons should be neverending. She mentioned that her new car had been bought with the proceeds of her latest novel. "With the proceeds of *my* last novel," he replied, "I purchased a small go-cart, or hand-barrow, on which my guests' luggage is wheeled from the station to my house. It needs a coat of paint. With the proceeds of my next I shall have it painted."

His situation was becoming worse, not better. In 1912, he had a horribly painful attack of shingles which completely prevented him from work. Edith and his friends became alarmed. In her concern for him, Edith was spurred to efforts which became embarrassing. In 1911, she had already made up her mind that James ought to get the Nobel Prize and had gone about it in the only way she knew, pressing the suggestion on various prominent people with the intention of having them influence the committee. Nothing came of this, but Edith was not deterred. In April, 1913, James had his seventieth birthday. His admirers in England had collected a considerable sum to pay for a portrait which should mark the occasion. Edith, rushing into the situation in March, decided that America owed him a present as well. As such, the notion was not unreasonable. James was the most distinguished of living American authors. He had long suffered from his lack of popular appeal. A gesture of appreciation at this point would be felt deeply as a justification of his lifework. Unfortunately the time was now too short to get a committee together, decide on the nature of the present, and do all things properly. Edith rushed out a leaflet signed only by herself appealing for money. This, being sent to James's American connections, soon came into the hands of his family. They were outraged. Not only had Edith suggested no use for the money, but she had mentioned a minimum sum of five thousand dollars. It looked to them as though she were holding out the hat for funds to support James during his old age. They protested hotly to James himself, who of course refused the money. The checks had to be returned, while Edith protested to the donors that she had been misunderstood.

Perhaps she had been so, but no one could deny that she had been injudicious. The appeal had indeed mentioned a gift and had suggested James should choose it. In fact, however, the disposal of the money would have been in her hands and his. There was nothing to prevent them spending part of it on a token and putting the rest into his bank account. The last-minute nature of the project and the absence of a committee did justify the protest of the Jameses.

Happily this incident did not disturb the friendship between Edith Wharton and James, who was far too generous to blame her for what had geen good intentions. This was indeed fortunate because, unknown to him, he had very great reason for being grateful to Edith. In the previous September when James was still struggling with his attack of shingles, in great pain and in a state of complete depression, Charles Scribner, the publisher, had written suggesting a new novel. He originally offered to buy it outright for eight thousand dollars, payable in advance. Later, he actually improved on this strangely generous offer, making the eight thousand dollars an advance on the American royalties. His motive, he admitted quite frankly, was to be of service to James. Perhaps he suggested that James, who had no descendants, might wish to enjoy in his lifetime the proceeds of a novel which might sell for generations. At all events, he must have put forward some pretext for a most unbusinesslike eagerness to give James money. At the very same moment he was with great reluctance parting with less than a third of this sum as advance on *two* books of reminiscences which James was preparing. He was pointing out to James's literary agent that he had not hitherto advanced over a thousand dollars to him—even on a novel. His caution is hardly surprising.

James's semi-annual royalty payment for the last six months had been less than two hundred dollars. The astounding thing is that Scribner found any pretext at all which could convince James that he was talking business.

James was not a practical man. He was ill and utterly depressed. What affected him at the moment more than the money was the thought that his publisher believed in him. He expanded, beginning as a natural result to believe in himself. The development was watched by Edith, who had been behind the negotiations, anxious that the written contract "give nothing away" and naturally indignant when James's agent, Pinker, claimed ten per cent of what was clearly her money. Exactly what the arrangement between herself and Scribner was, we may never know. But when the contract had been signed and the first four thousand paid over, she had her reward. She wrote to Scribner: "It was *very* kind of you to send me Mr. James's letter, and I am delighted at the complete success of the plan and warmly appreciative of all you have done. It did my heart good to read the letter."

Edith could afford the money. It was no great sacrifice to her. Remarkable, however, is the delicate, patient ingenuity by which she found the one way of helping James and persuaded Scribner, a kindhearted but scrupulous businessman, to act in it for her. In any case, James never finished the novel that he began. A fragment was

published after his death, underlining, if anything need
do so, the impractical nature of Scribner's arrangement.
Whatever was done, it was in part a tribute to Edith's
influence as Scribners' chief money-maker. This was all
the greater because a year or so earlier the connection
had suffered a shattering blow. Quite suddenly in her
usual fashion, Edith had signed a contract with the firm
of Appleton. Her reasons, as presented to her sorrowing
publisher, were unexceptionable. She could no longer
serialize her works in *Scribner's Magazine* as fast as she
could write them. She would continue with Scribners
as it suited her; but Appleton would place *The Reef*
with another magazine, then bring it out themselves.
More significantly, she had been offered most generous
terms.

An author has every right to do the best he can, and
the fact that Edith did not actually need money makes
no difference. But writing for money has its dangers
for a serious artist. There is nothing unworthy of Edith
in *The Reef*, which is beautifully written. A time was
to come, however, when the fact that she was pouring
out a series of second-rate books was largely concealed
by her financial profits. Appealing more and more steadily to people whose cultural level she despised, Edith
never understood that her work was becoming a contra-
diction in terms. Had she completely withdrawn from
money-making, she might more plausibly have claimed
the significance she craved as a critic of postwar morals

and manners. Attacking these in the language of soap opera or serial story, she was hopelessly lost. Her turn to Appleton marks no milestone in her life, yet it does underline the fact that she was up for sale. The rest would follow.

Not all the best works of these years were sold to the highest bidder. It was on a motor drive with a friend near Lenox that Edith had passed a battered old house, down-at-heel, unpainted, with a neglected yard, hens straggling over it, and ragged children sitting on the steps. "It is about a place like that," Edith told him, "that I mean to write a story. Only last week I went to the village meeting house in Lenox and sat there for an hour alone, trying to think what such lives would be, and some day I shall write a story about it." For the time being, she did not. Subjects for stories were apt to crowd into Edith's head so fast that she found it difficult to push them away and go on with what she was writing. Sometimes she actually did set aside what she was doing to outline or partly develop some new theme. Fairly often she kept an idea in mind and brooded on it while characters, names, and incidents gathered round it. The germ of *Ethan Frome* developed in this way. While Edith turned to other subjects, she kept her impression of the utter loneliness of the small villages in the Berkshire hills in the days before the coming of the motor. Eventually she took it up, and for a curious reason. She and Teddy gave up the New York house and started to winter regularly in Paris. Edith spoke French fluently, but not with the precision and aptness of an educated Frenchwoman. She started, therefore, to take conversation lessons, which soon included a written exercise. To Edith, a piece of writing must involve a story for her creative imagination to work on. Out of all the untouched plots that thronged her mind, she happened to pick out *Ethan Frome* to practice her French. Presently, she stopped her lessons for some reason or other and threw away her notebook. There for some little while the matter rested. Later, however, during a summer at "The Mount," the Berkshire scenery recalled her plot to mind. Next winter in Paris she wrote it, reading each day's work to Walter Berry in the evening and talking it over in detail, page by page.

Ethan Frome was not Edith's favorite work, yet she said about it that she was never conscious that she had mastered her craft until she wrote it. In truth, the construction of the story is superb. It is obvious to us that Edith had made up her mind to destroy Ethan before she even started. The theme of her tale and the mood in which it is written clearly demand this. Yet in other such stories where she piles agonies on top of a character previously doomed, we feel a slackening of suspense and also a touch of impatience with Edith. She exaggerates, we say to ourselves, and loses force. Not so with *Ethan Frome*. By letting us see Ethan after his tragedy from the first, she shifts our interest onto a different plane. We no longer imagine that she wants us to wonder whether he did make his escape from this grim and lonely New England township. Knowing he did not, we are prepared to let the curiosity of the narrator carry us quietly through the details of Ethan's story. At the ending, a final, savage twist lights up the whole in a single, lurid flash. The story of Ethan actually gains stature from the refinement of torture which Edith inflicts on him.

Equally remarkable is the written style. Clear, sensitive, musical, it never attracts attention to itself by cleverness, as Edith used to do. Everything fits the mood exactly, from the twisted apple trees in the orchard or the clear snow scene which greets the lovers to the sinister figure of Zeena's cat, symbolizing its mistress when Matt and Ethan are together. Even the dialogue, simple and unpretentious, suits the theme. Listen to Zeena: " 'It ain't done me a speck of good, but I guess I might as well use it up,' she remarked, adding as she pushed the empty bottle toward Mattie, 'if you can get the taste out, it'll do for pickles.' " This is the authentic twang of New England making itself heard—not too loudly, lest we lose the poetic qualities of the tale in the quaintness of a period, costume piece. Equally remarkable is the restraint with which Edith has refrained from drawing conclusions or moralizing on her theme. Ethan's own reticence is a true New England one and suits his story. Contrast her treatment of the theme in *Ethan Frome* with that of "Bunner Sisters," another long short story of considerable power.

Ann Eliza and Evelina Bunner run a tiny dressmaking and millinery shop in a shabby part of New York. Both fall in love with Mr. Ramy, a German clockmaker who is the first unmarried male to enter their lives. He prefers Ann Eliza, but her generous nature cannot bear to deprive the selfish Evelina of her hopes. She rejects Ramy and leaves him to her sister. What is the result? Ramy and Evelina grab Ann Eliza's savings, move to St. Louis, and disappear. Eventually Ann Eliza, lonely and on the verge of ruin, sees her sister return to die after being dragged by Ramy through the utmost depths of degradation. No touch is lacking to complete the tragedy of Ann Eliza's life. We finally see her tramping the streets of New York in search of a job, and we know she will not find one. What Edith wants to make us realize is that the sacrifice of happiness for another's sake by no means insures that we can pass that happiness on. Ann Eliza would willingly have died in a gutter for her sister. She was to do so, but without helping Evelina in the least.

Here we have two rather similar plots. Ethan Frome and his Mattie are trapped by Ethan's marriage to Zeena and the circumstances of their lives. We see the lovers as helpless victims of the grim side of New England life— harsh climate, poor soil, ill health, puritanism, remoteness. Edith's real concern is not their fate, but the forces which have destroyed them. Ann Eliza Bunner, after showing us something about the nature of sacrifice, is abandoned by her creator tramping the streets. Edith does not stoop to describe her wretched end. In fact, the events of both stories are conceived of as illustrations of a theme. Yet the accumulation of all possible misfortune on the head of Ann Eliza seems melodramatic. It does not convince us with the ease of *Ethan Frome* because it is not presented to us in such a masterly fashion. Nor can Edith leave us to draw our own conclusions. She draws them for us, though she does it well. "Self-effacement for the good of others had always seemed to her both natural and necessary; but then she had taken it for granted that it implied the securing of that good. Now she perceived that to refuse the gifts of life does not ensure their transmission to those for whom they have been surrendered; and her familiar heaven was unpeopled. She felt that she could no longer trust in the goodness of God, and that if he was not good he was not God, and there was only a black abyss above the roof of Bunner Sisters!" True, no doubt, but less effective than the stark simplicity of Ethan Frome calling daily at the post office, a connection with the outer world from which he never receives a communication. "Bunner Sisters" is a remarkable tale, but it is redeemed from melodrama only by the character of Ann Eliza, triumphantly vindicating human nature in the midst of crushing disaster.

Ethan Frome is indeed a masterpiece, but it has its weakness. Plain people have pointed out with a touch of impatience that the comprehension of the great lady of "The Mount" for local life has its limitations which cannot be overcome by sitting for an hour alone in the meeting house at Lenox. The criticism is valid. The gentle Ethan, too refined to push his love affair to any crude conclusion, is not a flesh-and-blood New England farmer. Edith hotly resented such remarks, though the truth is that she need not have done so. The problem of loneliness and isolation is a real one; and if Starkfield is rather an artist's painting than a photograph, is it the worse for that? Why should Edith aspire to realism when she has shown poetic insight?

Ethan Frome is perhaps the best single work Edith wrote in the prewar years, but it is not by any means her most ambitious effort. For all its perfection, it is a little thin compared to *The Custom of the Country*. This is another long, successful novel which deals with the society portrayed in *The House of Mirth*, though from a different point of view. The heroine this time is Undine Spragg from the Middle West, representative of the money-making crowd whose tasteless extravagance had destroyed the New York world of George and Lou. Sailing into New York with a determination to rise to the top of its social set, Undine captures Ralph Marvell, refined, blue-blooded, ineffective, and well-meaning. Of course she squeezes him like an orange, throws him away, and passes into the wealthy international set, where she marries a French marquis, one of the old conservative aristocracy of blood. She is no more able to put up with the restrictions of her position in France than she had been in New York. She is eventually matched with another of her own kind, only to be frustrated at last when she finds that he cannot rise to be an ambassador because she has been divorced. *The Custom of the Country* is a fascinating novel, well worth reading; but it foreshadows a development in Edith which was to produce inferior books. She was too good a hater. Critical she might be of the society into which she had been born; yet she admired it, appreciating its standards of personal integrity, conduct, or manners. For the wealthy newcomers to New York of her own generation, she felt nothing but outright loathing and contempt. One sees this in an anecdote preserved by a friend concerning an encounter in a European hotel:

"Mr. Wharton had preceded us after dinner to the hall, to order coffee and secure a comfortable corner, and when we followed we found him talking in the passage to two middle-aged ladies, clearly American. To my surprise Edith seemed not to perceive them, and she was passing without any sign of recognition when her husband called out, 'Oh, Pussy, don't you see the duchess?' Then indeed she did pause, gave a stiff bow in the direction of the group, and without further greeting proceeded, not to the hall but into the lift, beckoning to us to follow her. My husband did, but I lingered for a moment, desirous to see the end of the little scene. Mr. Wharton was all confused apology—that was easily seen. 'While she is taking the cure my wife,' he said, 'has to rest a great deal—she feels the cold, too.' 'Yes,' said the duchess serenely, 'I noticed the chill in the air.' Edith had swept the scene, but the duchess had certainly spoken the last word. In the Whartons' sitting-room the air was still a little chilly. 'Those dreadful women,' she said as her husband entered. 'We don't see them at home —why should we here?' " Truly the aristocrat is never afraid to be rude!

As Edith was in private life, so also was she towards her creation Undine Spragg. She gave her beauty and vitality, but could do no more. Undine's Middle Western parents whom she heartlessly despoiled were in situation at least a pathetic pair. Yet though she sees this, Edith has for them neither regard nor pity. They are monsters from a private Mars of her own, the world of commerce. With difficulty only does her imagination find them human. This is an extraordinary limitation of mind for a woman now well launched into the twentieth century and a native of the greatest commercial nation on earth. Nor is it as though she was universally cold to people who lived outside her small social circle. Everyone who knew her remarked on her tender intimacy with her servants. The fact is that for all her emancipation, there was still a great deal left in Edith Wharton of Lucretia

Rhinelander's little daughter, brought up to shine in her mother's old New York. All the standards of that day had been destroyed by the intrusion of tasteless wealth. Edith analyzed the process coolly, but her resentment was hotly personal. Later on, it was to betray her as an artist.

The Custom of the Country has another importance in Edith's development. It marks her continuing independence of Henry James and is the more significant because *The Reef*, published one year earlier, is unmistakably the work of James's disciple. His influence on her at that time was bound to be strong. It was not that they often discussed their works with each other. To Edith's clear mind, the cobweb subtleties of James's latest period were an irritation. It startled the great man's friends to see her gallop through his books without taking the time to weigh each word or fill out the hesitations of James's dialogue. She felt, moreover, that James's increasing emphasis on construction in his novels went too far. Posing a problem for his characters to solve, he tended to view them only as they wrestled with it, isolated from the world in some vague international setting, and divorced from any other relations or feelings. Yet James was far too sensitive to take her criticism well. When she voiced it, she only found she had hurt his feelings.

Edith's own nature was tougher than this. She always welcomed criticism from Walter Berry and might have done so equally from James. The difficulty here was that James did not wish to give it. On the subject of literary values he was incurably honest and far from sentimental. He thought Edith's work second-rate and was blind to some of her virtues which happened to differ from his own. If pressed for his opinion, he was capable of delivering it as follows: "Admirable, admirable; a masterly little achievement . . . Of course so accomplished a mistress of the art would not, without deliberate intention, have given the tale so curiously conventional a treatment. Though indeed, in the given case, no treatment *but* the conventional was possible; which might conceivably, my dear lady, on further consideration, have led you to reject your subject as—er—in itself a totally unsuitable one." In other words, he wanted to praise. He started to praise. His kindness of nature made it impossible that he should start in any other way. But he could not keep it up. The shout of laughter which greeted this particular sally merely emphasized his difficulty in talking to Edith about her art.

Directly, therefore, James rather tended to leave Edith's writing alone. But the rest of literature was open for their discussion. Both were literary craftsmen, interested in the techniques of storytelling and the refinements of style. It was only natural that they should dissect many models. It was inevitable, too, that Edith should be far more influenced than James. Her temperament was more receptive to outside hints; and she was younger, a comparative newcomer in the literary world. Besides, James's personality was always impressive. The remarkable thing is not that Edith borrowed so much from Henry James, but that she took so little. *The Reef*, to be sure, though beautifully written, is a pale reflection of his style. A romance between two middle-aged lovers is disturbed by the discovery that the governess, who is engaged to the lady's stepson, had previously had an affair with the man. All four characters, isolated in a French château, work out a personal problem much as the characters in James's *Golden Bowl* wrestle with the relations between the heroine's husband and her young stepmother. *The Custom of the Country* is refreshingly different from this. In construction, it follows the fortunes of the heroine, rather than working on a single, limited crisis. In tone it is a novel of social criticism like *The House of Mirth*. Instead of being, as is James's *Golden Bowl*, divorced from its surroundings, *The Custom of the Country* depends on them. They are its subject. Undine and her husbands, French or American, represent their backgrounds. The conflict is fought between social groups rather than people.

The Custom of the Country rounded out Edith's great creative period. It was now 1913, and within a twelvemonth that rich and pleasant world to which she had the key would vanish forever. For a few brief years she had been the brilliant Mrs. Wharton, lifted by wealth and talent into the company of those select few who led

Western culture. Not merely through James, but in her own right she had become a person whose mere presence conferred an honor. The list of her friends reads like a private *Who's Who* of her times. Her travels to London, Paris, Italy, North Africa, Spain became actually dizzying to follow. No wonder Henry James christened her "the pendulum woman," never still. Who was now the real Edith, that restless, famous woman, or shy little Miss Jones who had married Teddy? In fact, what had happened to Edith's inner nature? Had she actually become no more than a sounding board for bright ideas?

Chapter 6

FRENCH WAYS

Paris is a city of enduring charm. It has long been the fashion to talk of Paris as though it were the spiritual capital of Europe. Before the First World War, this may have done less than justice to the gay if decadent Vienna; to Rome, center of an artistic tradition and an age-old church; to ugly commercial and military Berlin; or to London, whence the Mother of Parliaments dominated her vast empire. Yet Paris in some degree had all their virtues. Capital city of a rich and gifted people, Paris had its own gaiety, its schools of painting, its commerce, its strong political passions, and even its relics of military glory, the more attractive because they really belonged to the distant past. Its physical appearance was worthy of its greatness. For many centuries the first city in Europe, Paris was lovely before the industrial age. The nineteenth century had made its additions, including the monstrosity of the Eiffel Tower. But whereas London had grown in any way, the center of Paris had been saved by the genius of the great Napoleon and by the interest in planning which he had inspired. To the modern visitor, Paris is a city of beautiful vistas. The foreign resident knows its quaint corners and unexpected trees. The Frenchman, though aware of occasional squalor, considers his city the center of the earth.

His reasons for doing so are historical ones. In the nineteenth century, brilliant exiles from other lands had foregathered in Paris. It had suited King Louis-Philippe, the French Republic, and even to some extent Napoleon III to give asylum to foreign liberals. The government of England, to be sure, was still more tolerant; but British people were notorious for their coldness to strangers. Strong personalities like Marx and Lenin lived many years in London without making the slightest impression on the natives. London, in fact, was exile indeed. Paris was the place where people met to discuss their ideas. Paris truly had been the nineteenth-century center of Europe. Her position in the twentieth, when Edith Wharton knew her best, was beginning to change.

There were, to start with, fewer leaders of foreign thought in Paris. Liberalism and parliaments of a sort had come into fashion. It was possible to oppose one's government and remain at home. The consolidation of the German Empire had presented Europe with a rival focus. The unification of Italy had given significance to Rome. Europe was grouping itself into larger areas, preparing itself in fact for World War I. Coming events were casting their shadow. It is strange that Edith, who had made her debut in the vanishing world of old New York, now came to Paris once more at the eleventh hour. Immersed in her personal troubles, busy with her travels, concerned with her friends and her French lessons, Edith hardly saw the signs of the times. It was not surprising. Very few comprehended the shape of things to come.

Teddy's health had not improved with the years. Little is known about mental diseases today, and less was known then. The strains of the Wharton's marriage had been greatly increased by Edith's rise to fame. Perhaps unconsciously Teddy was taking his revenge on her—perhaps not. At all events, early in 1908 he had a serious attack of gout, accompanied by another nervous breakdown. It was too cold for Aix, so he sailed for America to take a cure at Hot Springs. Edith did not go with him. The doctors felt they were better apart. She joined him in the early summer at Lenox, when she found him recovered. Hot Springs had done him a world of good—"given him new hands and new feet." His spirits had returned to normal, and he entertained her hugely with descriptions of the rich Middle Westerners who had practically taken over Hot Springs. But by the end of the summer, the nervous strain was reappearing; and by January he had broken down again. This time it was not so easy to put him on his feet. In addition, the life of the Whartons was now complicated by the fact that his physical health seemed to be bettered by regular cures at Hot Springs, while hers depended on Salso Maggiore. By August, Teddy was no better. Edith was close to despair. Her husband was not completely irresponsible, but his condition varied. For a short visit, he might even appear quite normal. She found it, however, impossible to give her attention to running the house or the place. He took all her time.

For years, change of scene had seemed to do Teddy good; and the frantic pace of the Whartons' travel was partly at least on his account. Doctors had forbidden the winters in New York, and the Whartons had agreed to take an apartment in Paris, whence a dash to the south of France in search of warmer weather might occasionally serve to raise Teddy's spirits. The choice of Paris as a second home seems to have been his as much as hers. He did not like England, where in any case the winter is depressing. Their acquaintance with the Bourgets had made them familiar with a Paris group. Edith's mother had died in Paris in 1900, and her brother Harry was living there still. As traveled people, they were aware of the city's special charm. Besides, Parisians have wide-ranging interests. Not everybody has intellectual tastes or wants to indulge in them to the exclusion of all else. Teddy by nature was a pleasant man with social instincts. He and Edith had to some extent enjoyed the same friends for twenty years. It was natural for them now to try and go on.

Very likely, trouble had increased because living in Paris was not the same thing as visiting there. Edith herself had felt her fluent French inadequate to new demands. The Whartons had to take their place in French society; and they found this different from being occasional visitors who spoke French well. Helped by her abilities, her friends, her fame, Edith had made the adjustment. Teddy could not. He never quite fitted in. No doubt this played a part in his deterioration.

By 1911, things were so intolerable during the summer at Lenox that Edith packed her trunk and departed for Newport. Immediately Teddy wanted her back, appealed for help to his brother, and precipitated a big family row. Matters were eventually patched up. Teddy had been loudly complaining to all who would hear that Edith had deprived him of the management of "The Mount" and of their money. Now at least, he seemed to perceive that his behavior had gone too far; and he made a great effort to pull himself together. Really encouraged for the first time in three years, Edith consented to give him back control of affairs at "The Mount." One of his impulses had been to sell the place, get rid of the responsibility. Edith, who felt strongly that he needed the quiet and the rest of a country summer, argued against this. In September, she sailed for Europe, leaving him to enjoy the shooting, take his Hot-Springs cure, and rejoin her later on. Meanwhile, he promised that he would not sell "The Mount" without due consultation. But so uncon-

trolled by now were his vagaries that the solemn agreement meant nothing. He sold "The Mount" while she
was still on the ocean and sent a cable announcing he had
done so.

Edith hid her troubles from all but a few. To James
she wrote more fully. His letters, which hitherto had
started formally "Dear Edith and Edward," or at the
least had sent Teddy his regards, now cease once and
for all to mention his name. What he could say to con-
sole Edith in her trouble, James said. But there was nothing that he or anyone could do of practical use. Teddy
did not improve. By 1912, Edith had persuaded him to
enter a luxurious private sanitarium on Lake Constance.
In 1913, she divorced him, "for her own protection,"
friends say. Poor Teddy remained in a sanitarium all
through the war, but was taken back to America in 1918
by his sister, who cared for him until her death. Teddy
lingered another six years and died in 1928, having been,
as Edith said, hardly alive for many years.

None of these adjustments were made without pain.
In particular, the Wharton family, to whom she had
never felt close, did not like the divorce. They may have
taken the view that, since there were no children to be
considered, Edith's first concern should always have
been Teddy. Most certainly they did not see as early or
as clearly as Edith did that it was essential for him to
have specialist care. Such family differences of view
in tragic cases are common enough. The situation, how-

ever, might have been eased for Edith if the members of her own family had backed her up. Unfortunately, with the single exception of her sister-in-law, nobody did. Her brother Freddy, after nearly thirty years of marriage, had run off in 1896 with another woman. Minnie Jones had divorced him; and the circumstances of the whole case had been such that everyone's sympathies had been with her. Edith, who had always been especially devoted to Minnie, had become yet further embroiled with Fred a few years later when Lucretia's will was found to discriminate unfairly against her daughter. In fact, communications had been broken off. In 1918, Fred died obscurely in New York, and none of his countless cousins went to the funeral. Edith's letters duly appeared on black-bordered paper, but she actually apologized to Minnie for going through this form. One could not—one simply could not mourn for Freddy.

Harry, who always had been Edith's favorite brother, was living in Paris at the time of Edith's troubles and her divorce. He was, however, growing more and more eccentric and fell eventually into the power of a woman of whom his relatives with one accord disapproved. He died in 1922, according to legend, starved to death by his wife's pathological desire to economize. At all events, though he had lived for very many years in the same city as Edith, he had flatly refused to see her and visited his anger on anyone who attempted to bring them together. Either for this reason, or possibly also out of genuine affection for Teddy, he did not take Edith's part. It happened, moreover, that in 1913 at the time of Edith's divorce, Harry was very ill.

For all these reasons, in the crisis of her life, Edith stood unsupported. She had undoubtedly been a demanding wife, and the very imperfections of her relationship with Teddy made it difficult for her to confide in others freely. Yet with all the force of her nature and with the strongest sense of obligation, she really had done her best. To make her situation even more pitiable, these years of strain coincided with suffering of another sort. After more than twenty years of married frustration, Edith at last had fallen in love with somebody else.

She had known Walter Berry well for about twenty years. We have seen how he had originally helped her with *The Decoration of Houses* and how she discussed with him the manuscript of *Ethan Frome,* which was written in these years of terrible trouble. It had long been established that Walter Berry was her literary adviser. Always over-anxious and lacking in self-confidence, Edith had used him as a sounding board. To his critical intelligence she attributed the perfecting of her style. To his understanding of the great masters of literature, she owed the deepening and enriching of her work. Walter Berry, son of a New York Van Rensselaer, born in Paris, counsel for the French and Italian Embassies in Washington, shared with her that cultivated background which she valued in her life above all else. In fact, it had

long been obvious that Walter Berry held a special place
in her life, different for instance from that occupied by
Henry James, and different from Teddy's. Walter Berry
was the "soul-mate" described in her short story of long
ago, "The Fullness of Life." Why then, one may rea-
sonably ask, did she fall in love with him at the age of
forty-six and not before?

She came in the first place of a social group which
took marriage with the utmost seriousness. As we have
seen, she could write stories of divorce without con-
demning the women who deserted their dull husbands.
Yet her attitude is best defined by a brilliant story called
"Autres Temps" which she published early in the war.
Mrs. Lidcote ran away from her husband with another
man, and she became a social outcast. The loss of friends
and positions soured her lover in spite of himself. By the
time the story opens, he is dead. Mrs. Lidcote has been
living obscurely in Europe, only visiting New York in
strictest privacy now and again to see her daughter. Suddenly the daughter follows her mother's example and
deserts her husband for a new lover. Mrs. Lidcote rushes
across to stand by her. She arrives to find the whole
problem simply settled. Everyone has had a quick divorce and is remarried. Society no longer cares in the
least. She soon discovers, however, that her own position is unchanged. People have pretty well forgotten
what she did; but they know that nobody has spoken to

her in twenty years and are too lazy to think her case through again. She actually has to have dinner sent up on a tray because the friends of her daughter will not meet her. Mrs. Lidcote prepares to return to Europe and obscurity. As she does so, she reflects that all the suffering inflicted on her by past or present injustice has given her a source of strength which her daughter lacks. In spite of everything, she prefers a kind of world in which conduct has rules.

As she prefers it, so does Edith. Marriage may be broken, but never lightly and never without loss. For all his deficiencies, Teddy had loved her and been infinitely kind. At the end of "The Fullness of Life," the woman sat waiting for the commonplace husband who adored her. Edith for many years had accepted her husband, filling up her emptiness with friends, of whom Berry was chief.

In some such fashion Edith had staved off love, or at all events she had not abandoned herself to it wholly. Perhaps, had not Teddy failed her, she might have kept her head. It is significant that the time of her surrender was not that of Teddy's first breakdown or even of his second, but of his third, which had finally convinced her that the disease was inherited and incurable. His illness hit her in a private part of her life which very few were ever able to penetrate deeply. It is remarkable that though one may see her views on love and marriage outlined in much of what she wrote, one hardly traces the slightest contact with the problems of the unconscious self or the toppling reason.

The nearest she comes is in her ghost stories. Like James, Edith was a mistress of the unsensational ghost story in a modern setting whose thrill depends on an unusual combination of the ordinary with the eerie. Rather occasionally, her stories touch as though by coincidence on the unconscious self. The best example, and one of her very good ghost stories, is "The Eyes," which she must have written not too long after Teddy's third breakdown.

Culwin, an elderly roué, has gathered about him a group of younger men for the pleasure of basking in their unsophisticated admiration. To the youngest and most innocent of these, and in the presence of the narrator, he is induced to talk about an experience which affects him strangely. At certain crises of his life when he has performed an act which he thinks unselfish, but which we perceive is not so, he has been haunted by a pair of terrible eyes. They are evil, elderly, dissipated; and they afflict him with a sense of special horror. Eventually he sees by the expression on his protegé's face, and then in a mirror behind him, that the eyes are now his own, reflecting what he has made of himself through his long lifetime.

No closer does Edith come, even in the years of crisis, to the hidden tragedies of a damaged spirit. But at this time she turned to Walter Berry with a passion in strange contrast to her former control. She could no longer live without him. Teddy's incomprehension of her deepest needs had become unbearable. She was by turns passionate and despairing. She provided no answer to her problem, still feeling trapped by her marriage, though its conditions had become intolerable. She only looked to Berry to give her a signal.

It was not given. In 1908, the very year of Teddy's breakdown and of Edith's love and anguish, Walter Berry accepted the post of a judge on the International Tribunal in Cairo. He departed for Egypt with his widowed sister to keep house for him, leaving Edith to manage her affairs as best she might. In some respects this was only honorable and prudent. A lifelong bachelor, Berry did not intend to marry Edith. Nor did he ever do so. At the time of her divorce, he was living in Paris, having retired from the International Court. He did not marry her then. When he died in 1927, he was still as intimate with her as he had ever been, but still unmarried.

It is a curious love-history which suggests that Walter Berry was a peculiar man. If he had loved but renounced Edith, he would have married her on her divorce. If he did not love her, then his behavior was strange indeed. For twenty years he had been willing to play the "soul-mate," yet he could not be brought to undertake the marriage. Edith and he had always had a great deal in common. Even more than Henry James, he shared her tastes and background. An omnivorous reader with a fine critical mind, he thrilled to beauty in literature or art as did Edith herself. Internationally cultured, he was friends with great men, among whom one may specially mention Henry James and Marcel Proust. As a lawyer, he was distinguished. As a rich man, he was a true patron of the arts. But a number of people, including some of Edith's friends, actively disliked him.

They thought him a narrow-minded snob and deplored his influence on Edith as the worst possible. Dismissing her contention that he showed her how to write, they claim her abilities and interests would have taught her this without him. As for his influence on her spirit, they attribute to Berry all that was hardest and least attractive about Edith. As we have seen, despite her quick sympathies, Edith could judge on the basis of a cut-and-dried set of standards. Berry, some felt, had encouraged this habit, and not merely in the world of continental hotels. Politically Berry was a rigid reactionary and influenced Edith, who respected his judgment as a man of affairs. He was, moreover, one of those people to whom speculation about the deeper meaning of life, about religion or mysticism are nonsense. In his lifetime, Edith would brush off these categories of experience without discussion. In sum, a few people felt she would have been better without him. It was her tragedy that she had to expend her deepest feelings on a man too selfish to return them. Of course it dried up tenderness within her, made her, that woman of many friends, so hard to know well.

This much friends have said. It is fair to add that Edith loved Walter Berry all her life and never suggested that he failed her or that she saw the limitations which other people pointed out. Her generosity overlooked the way she was treated, if indeed it was unfairly. She kept her secret and he his. But we do know that she suffered, that she envied people who had been happy with a deep inner contentment which she felt was denied her.

Edith buried her hurt feelings very deep. Once in a single brief sentence she broke out to a friend, only to ignore that fact thereafter for twenty-five years. Some people have felt that there is a trace of Walter Berry in the cultured, selfish dilettantes who appear in her stories, now as hero, now as villain. Certainly the type is a persistent one, ranging from Selden, too self-absorbed to save Lily Bart, as far as to Culwin, the elderly roué of "The Eyes." There is in fact a more terrible character still, in the story, "After Holbein." Old Anson Warley, who was once a cultured man with ideas and aspirations, has been for many years a mere diner-out. Tottering at the point of death in a moment of mental aberration, he enters the house of Mrs. Jaspar (a thin disguise for Mrs. William Astor). Mrs. Jaspar, formerly a leader of the vulgarly splendid set, still dresses up—or thinks she does—in all her jewels to receive imaginary guests. She receives Warley, and the two partake of a grisly feast of which the wine is water, the flowers are newspapers stuffed in a bowl, the food is spinach and served in kitchen crockery. The scene is a terrible one in which the nearness of approaching death is shown in fearful contrast to the values and preoccupations of these lost souls. "After Holbein," is Edith's ultimate criticism of mere social values. One could say no more. If there is in it also a trace of resentment against the bachelor who steadily refused to be involved in loving and living, one can only say that Anson Warley is by no means Walter Berry. Yet over and over again that streak of selfishness persists in Edith's men. Where did she meet it? Not in Teddy, nor in George Frederic Jones, one may imagine. Was it in her brothers? Or perhaps after all she did see something in Berry which her creative self could criticize, though she still adored the man.

So much went on in Edith's life during those crowded years before the First World War. In artistic achievement, she reached a climax. She was never later to write so well over such a long period or in so many ways. In her private life she made both an end and a beginning. Teddy's sale of the Lenox house had severed ties which she did not knit up again. It was a natural thing for her to resign herself. Associations were bound to have been painful at "The Mount," while her unaided fortune might well have been unequal to its expense. "The Mount," moreover, had always been especially Teddy's.

He had loved the Berkshires as the scenes of his boyhood. Edith, though she had enjoyed the countryside, made few friends there. In fact, she had hated paying calls and had pronounced the neighbors an exceedingly dull lot. "The XYZs," she informed her own guests as she returned from one duty visit, "have made up their minds that they will have *books* in their library!" The Berkshire scenery inspired her to write *Ethan Frome* and a later companion piece called *Summer*. The Berkshire residents of her own class inspired her in nothing.

Detached, then, from Lenox, Edith felt rootless in America at large. Newport was distasteful to her. New York, sadly changed from the past, was also dull. Besides, as Edith began to contemplate divorce, she must have felt that it would raise barriers there. The remnants of her old exclusive set looked down on divorce, and Edith was far too proud to explain or be forgiven. In fact, her life in America had come to an end, at least for a time. Having wintered in Paris for a good many years, she thought it natural to remain in France, or at any rate in Europe for a few summers as well. She had made a place for herself in Paris society and felt at home. America for a while at least meant memories of Teddy.

It is never easy to adapt oneself to life in a foreign country. Unlike most Americans who have settled in Paris since, Edith really aspired to be in a certain sense French. Without severing her international connections, she wanted to be accepted in French society for herself, not just as a foreigner. And being Edith, by French Society, she meant the best.

Parisian society as Edith knew it offered a strange combination of intellectual freedom and social snobbery. Like Paris itself, it had been largely shaped in the preceding century. Since Napoleon, France had had four regimes: the Bourbon monarchy, the more liberal Orleanist one, the empire of Napoleon III, and the French Republic. This last, which had held power for nearly forty years, was by now firmly established. One should not, however, for this reason suppose that influential people supported it with any particular pleasure. Middle-class democracy held no appeal for the inheritors of the great aristocratic names or for the owners of the industrial fortunes which had dominated the mid-nineteenth century. With one accord the upper classes preferred the old days, differing merely in the epoch they looked back to. The gulf between them and the present regime had been widened by the secular constitution of the Republic, which outraged the fervently Catholic aristocrats and even in many respects the Bonapartists. Political feeling, always intense in France, had been raised to a white-hot heat at the end of the century by the impact of the Dreyfus case in 1894. Alfred Dreyfus, an army officer, a Jew, and therefore in the opinion of his better-born colleagues not a gentleman, had been accused of espionage and convicted on the flimsiest evidence. It had been convenient, and certain people conducting the inquiry had been stupid. Once done, the injustice was by no means easily redressed. The honor of the Army was involved, and the fate of Major Dreyfus became a focus for the hatreds engendered by the revolutions of the past hundred years. The position of the aristocrat, the military caste, the Catholic faith, the Jew, the very nature of the Republic itself obscured the issue of a simple act of justice. In 1906 the Dreyfus case was ended; but its influence lingered on. In drawing-room circles politics were no longer discussed. They simply could not be if people were to keep their tempers. The politicians of the Republic had their own social groups where they could make their deals or jostle for power. The aristocracy, powerless, deeply divided, yet at one in their disgust had turned away.

The old-style aristocrats had taken refuge in narrow exclusiveness. They had transferred loyalty from the State to the Family in its widest sense. Though they were a declining class, many of them were still wealthy with big ancestral estates and enormous "hotels" in the Faubourg St. Germain of Paris. These latter were built around pleasant formal gardens and entered through magnificent wrought-iron gates and cobbled courtyards. To some extent their glory had departed. Outer courtyards and often inner ones as well had been converted into flats. The Family, however, ignoring and indeed despising their tenants, still inhabited the recesses of their house. Here they received their own connections and entertained as widely as their means would permit. But though courteous to inferiors, society condescended to all whose blood did not run equally blue.

Such people may not appear worth knowing. Indeed in many cases they were haughty, dowdy, self-centered, old-fashioned, and dull. No doubt their position was a familiar one to Edith, who could sympathize with their lot. But if she had wanted exclusive dullness, she could have stayed in New York. Why bother to penetrate such a very closed circle? She did, in fact, possess a key to it. When she had been wintering in Cannes with her dying father, she had gone everywhere with two young French girls and their American mothers. They had never forgotten her and gladly welcomed her now. The door was open, but was it really worth her while to enter in?

Strangely enough, she found it so. The aristocratic tradition of the old families of France was far more securely based in the past than was that of George and Lou. It stood for a continuity in French history as a whole. Edith's long devotion to the treasures of the past could as it were be embodied in the survival of this old, distinguished group. Nor was it by any means entirely boring. Despising politics and money-making, the more able had turned to culture of the mind. The Comtesse de Noailles, for instance, was a distinguished poetess and to Edith one of the most fascinating women she had ever met. Edith's instinct for associating with those at the top was more than snobbery. The Faubourg St. Germain contained many people whom she enjoyed. It entertained others, for the more intelligent sought their own kind among the intellects of Paris. Now and then as a foreigner Edith found herself impatient with the formal outward conventions which were the price of being accepted. On one occasion, she remarked, when she first lived in Paris, she wanted to give a dinner party to various people who had been conspicuously kind. But French society had its elaborate rules of precedence and seating, the host in the middle of the table and the company tapering to the less distinguished ends. The ramifications of precedence were infinite, depending on antiquity of title, degree of cousinage, intermarriage at some obscurely distant point, and overridden by counterclaims like those, for instance of bishops or members of the Académie Française. Uncertain how to arrange her table and unwilling to be thought ignorant, Edith consulted a French friend who threw up her hands at the complications involved and went to ask one of her uncles, an authority on just this kind of thing. She returned with the old duke's verdict on the seating and his hopes that the arrangement would do. He added, however, that in fact these particular people never ought to be asked to dinner together. They were excellent friends and met one another often, but the question of precedence in their case was so delicate that they really could not dine in company. Any foreigner who wants to be accepted by a group must be so on its own terms, however ridiculous. Edith might smile, but she submitted to conventions of no particular value which were not native to her.

The Faubourg St. Germain by no means represented the cream of Paris in a true intellectual sense. In the university world of the Sorbonne Edith also made many friends. She found, however, the society of specialists boring unless they happened to be art historians. What was worse, the Parisian *savant* had seldom much to say to a woman. After dinner, the learned men would get together over coffee and cigars, while their much less interesting wives tried to cope with Edith by asking stupid questions like: "Do you write all your books in French and then have them translated into English?" The good ladies were dying, or so at least Edith felt, to gossip about the comfortable subjects of children, sickness, and servants. A lady authoress with a forbidding expression dried up their normal flow and left them tongue-tied.

Far more congenial to Edith was the society of Jacques-Emile Blanche, a distinguished painter and anglophile, in whose company the artistic and literary worlds of Paris and London happily blended. The Blanches entertained an informal, sometimes a Bohemian group of serious artists. The great sensation of the pre-war years was Diaghilev's creation of the Russian ballet in Paris, drawing on the talents of Stravinsky and a number of distinguished modern artists, including Picasso. Artistically, Paris was moving into the twentieth century ahead of the rest of the world. At the Blanches' in the company of Diaghilev and other leaders of new trends, Edith met writers of a very different sort from herself. André Gide, for instance, had spent his literary career in denouncing the conventional morals which conflicted with the tendencies of his private life. Edith, who in general upheld conventional standards, was quite prepared to accept Gide as a serious writer. She was sensitive to his personal charm and also to that of Jean Cocteau, an even wilder rebel who was to make a sensation in the postwar world when Gide already seemed conservative and out of date. In other words, among the creative artists to whom Edith's talents had by now introduced her, she beheld with tolerant eyes. Edith Wharton was never truly a twentieth-century character herself, but she was intelligent; and literature in France is intellectual. Here was a chance for her to grow, lose her rigidities, and accept the coming of a new age. It coincided aptly with the growth of a new life, independent of Teddy and even to some extent of Walter Berry. Edith needed in a very real sense to catch up with the world. Unhappily the sands of time were running out fast. In 1911, 1912, or 1913, few suspected what a short while there was left for the old way of living.

Such were the groups that made up Edith's Paris, di-

versified by many guests and transatlantic callers. All
these elements, however, were brought together and
blended by a unique institution peculiar to France, the
Paris *salon*. Fundamentally a *salon* is a group of congenial people who meet in pleasant surroundings to talk
over subjects which interest them. Other nations may
have their discussion groups, scientific or literary clubs.
These are not *salons*. A *salon* depends in the first place
on a hostess and a social situation. It is talk in a drawing-
room atmosphere, relaxed yet learned. It is talk for in-
formation, yet even more strongly for the simple pleasure of good talk. Rarely is anyone allowed a monologue.
If a man cannot develop his theme through the tossing
of ideas back and forth by the group, then he does not
belong in the *salon*, but in the lecture hall. One expects
from a *salon* enlightenment rather than learning, a new
view of something, not a report or a study. Its pleasure
is found in the direct meeting of minds, not in the im-
provement of their knowledge of solid fact. The art of
conversation is one few people bother to learn well, but
those who do so find themselves infinitely rewarded. It
is especially the field of the gifted amateur like Edith,
whose studies of art and history had always been directed by conversation with others. In the French *salon*
there is a sense of amateur effort, inevitably so, since it
is the creation of a woman who devotes her time to entertaining.

It would be a mistake to suppose that any wealthy

hostess with a good cook and comfortable chairs could gather a *salon* by simply inviting her guests to come and talk. A true *salon* is built around a permanent group. Its continuity insures its individual character. Some *salons*, it is true, have non-resident members who are welcomed when they come to Paris. Guests are common, but the members of the inner group remain the same. Some *salons* are built round an individual, like the famous *salon* run in the nineties around Anatole France. Some are literary, some artistic, some political. All contain men and women, with the difference that it is on the whole the men who air their views, while the women are expected to draw them out. This is a task which needs real understanding of any subject which may happen to be touched on.

Any hostess who intends to run a *salon* must give her time to it. She has, in the first place, to collect her group of congenial people who can draw one another out. This may not be easy, since the aspiring hostess has rivals. Assuming, however, that her *salon* becomes established, she must always be on the alert for new blood, not in quantities, lest she change the character of the group, yet not in too small doses either. Nothing could be more dreary than the little gatherings which have met weekly in the same drawing room for fifty years, their members too prosy to be accepted elsewhere and too familiar to strike the smallest spark out of one another. In order to attract newer talent and have a reservoir of occasional guests, the hostess must entertain widely. Besides her weekly luncheons or dinners for the inner group, she must have larger gatherings regularly at which she meets the whole world, or rather that part of it which suits her *salon*, political, musical, or whatever it may be. The selection of women for her group will be a special problem. They will be expected to cap quotations, answer like a flash, comprehend any subject, and radiate feminine charm. For herself, she must be master of her subjects, read all the latest books, see all the plays, hear all the new music, be primed with all gossip about the latest trends, read all the papers and periodicals of a serious sort, see the new art exhibits, and take an interest in all current subjects, be they discoveries of archaeological treasures in Egypt or the philosophical conception of the nature of time put forth by M. Bergson. Too superficial a knowledge of these subjects will not do. She will have, after all, to direct the conversation unobtrusively and see it goes well, that nobody dominates it too long and that when a subject has been thrashed out, it naturally leads to another.

The life of a *salon* leader was just as full of writing notes, keeping engagements, or snapping up distinguished guests as that of a hostess in any other city. It naturally required for outstanding success a handsome fortune, since good food and wine attracted people or served to keep them coming. But the *salon*, which was the real purpose behind entertaining, lent it a special

flavor. People of brilliance, intellectual or artistic leaders, were the guests around whom hostesses planned their
evenings. The aristocratic set, though by no means ignored, was mainly valued because its leisure had allowed
it to cultivate talents. Though the old families as a group
held aloof from the world, individual members with
special interests either ran their own *salons* or attended
those of others where they expected to meet interesting
persons. In other words, there was more intercourse between the various leading groups in Paris society than
might have been expected. The political life of the great
capital impinged mainly on the political *salons*. But cultural life in every form was the true concern of Paris.
On cultural issues people could safely fight battles with
true Parisian violence, adopt causes, argue, divide, and
come together again. All the excitement stored up by
deep inner divisions in French life found an outlet here.
In no other city was so much passion expended on ideas,
so comparatively little on political issues. Here people's
prejudices too often prevented the raising of political
subjects at all.

The widowed Comtesse Robert de Fitz-James, to
whom Edith was introduced by Paul Bourget, occupied
a halfway position between the old families of Paris and
the new. She was in origin an Austrian Jewess from a
famous Viennese banking family, but she had married
early, always lived in Paris, and associated with the right
families, though a few of the purest aristocrats raised

eyebrows at her. Mme. de Fitz-James received her guests
in three drawing rooms of varying sizes, by no means
specially distinguished and yet housing fine collections
of eighteenth-century furniture and rare books. Here
every week she had a dinner for fourteen or sixteen, followed by a larger reception. Her real intimates were invited on another evening for a smaller dinner or to an
informal lunch on Fridays, when she served two exquisite menus of meat and fish. So fascinating was the conversation that more than once Edith absentmindedly ate
both and found that other people fell into the same error.
Completely devoted to the life of her own *salon*, Mme.
de Fitz-James seldom dined out. Her parties were
blended with exquisite care. To the inner circle, Edith
was soon added. Her talents and background made the
group a natural one for her. The *salon* of Mme. de Fitz-
James included, besides Paul Bourget, a number of the
most distinguished poets, playwrights, and novelists of
the hour, a few well-known scholars, and—a tribute to
the cosmopolitan origins of Mme. de Fitz-James—diplo-
mats. A number of these were Frenchmen stationed
abroad and thus only occasional visitors in Paris. Others,
however, included the German, Austrian, and Argen-
tinian ambassadors and one of the attachés of the British
Embassy. Well-known newspapermen renowned for
their wit earned a place at the table ends furthest from
the hostess, where the less distinguished of the company

were placed. Men outnumbered women and led the talk, but among the latter were the daughter and sister of famous poets as well as a number of brilliant foreigners. Once Edith's own position was established, she made additions to the company from among her own regular guests—Bernard Berenson, Walter Berry, and Henry James.

Thus Edith settled down to her new life amid the society of all that was most congenial to her. She still traveled a great deal in the summers, visited England, made a flying trip to Germany, toured Spain, once actually inducing Rosa de Fitz-James, lame though she was, to come with her. She had a particularly enchanting holiday in Sicily and for the first time made acquaintance with the North African desert. Its limitless horizons overwhelmed the restless, anxious woman who in general preferred what men had made out of a landscape to seeing it untouched. Her friends—for of course she traveled with friends—saw her briefly hushed and at peace. There was talk of returning; but already, alas, it was the spring of 1914.

In this sort of way Edith passed through the transition from America to Europe. Everything urged her in the same direction, her lack of sympathy for the commercial life of New York, the breakdown of her marriage, growing friendship with Henry James and his literary circle in England, life in Paris, and the fascinating companionship of people who were her equals in talent, wit, or culture. Yet there was a danger that in gaining so much she might lose more. For a woman who had married and had loved, Edith's private life was singularly barren. Lacking husband, children, roots, she was now adapting herself with skill to ways which were not hers. They were never quite to become so. Edith's French, for instance, was as fluent as her English; but her accent was never perfect and her written style lacked all the distinction of her work in her own language. In other words, Edith was not French, nor had she even settled as early abroad as Henry James. Her novels and stories are not, like those of James, detached from a national scene. They are about America as Edith knew it and about the social conditions which she saw there. How could she transfer this sort of thing to Paris? What enrichment of her real background did she gain from the cosmopolitan talk of the Fitz-James *salon?* Henry James himself had seen this very much earlier and had stated that Edith must be "tethered in her own back yard." But now that he knew her well, understood her sufferings of these past years, and saw her thrill to the stimulus of all this brilliant talk, he either had not the heart to repeat himself or, if he did so, never really urged her to take up life in America again. Edith as author and Edith as woman were at variance still. They had always been so; yet hitherto the author had reached out hungrily, while the woman had lived with Teddy in Newport or

Lenox. Now it was the woman who enjoyed herself in Paris, while the author, her roots cut off, might be in danger of withering away. Yet how could anyone grudge her intellectual satisfaction? Had she not earned it by her own unaided efforts? What else had she?

Chapter 7

WAR YEARS

EDITH'S new life took shape in the Rue de Varenne, where her modern apartment looked out over a huddle of ancient buildings. In apartment terms, as even Edith admitted in a rare moment of financial uncertainty, it was large. It had to be, since her style of living was imposing. There was White, the English butler, presiding with a dignified air over the establishment. There was Mrs. White. There was Cook, the monumental chauffeur, magnificently unconcerned by Edith's constant fussing about his route, the map, strange sounds in the motor—all devices by which she made up for having to leave the driving to somebody else. There was Gross, the personal maid, a simple and beautiful character, completely devoted to her mistress and the spoiled little dogs. There were various housemaids and a cook. And there was Anna.

Anna Bahlmann, of German-American stock, had been Edith's governess, one of the few people who had appreciated and fed her growing intelligence. Anna had gone on to other jobs; but she was now old and her savings were not adequate. Edith had coaxed her to come back and help her. Unhappily, Anna was fiercely independent; and it was necessary to persuade her that she really earned her keep. She could not type well, since her fingers were too rheumatic. She could not take dictation either, save slowly in longhand. At one moment Edith had the brilliant thought of putting her in charge of the household books. But when Anna beheld the size of the monthly bills and counted the number of Edith's other dependents, she was so horrified that she refused a salary. This would not do, and something else had to be thought of. Edith found a market at Scribners for a translation of Anna's from the German, which she touched up herself to improve its style. Anna ran little errands, wrote a few business letters. In fact, her occupations were planned with patient care. Anna, meanwhile, was highly difficult. Her memory was not what it was, and she was growing deaf. Yet fiercely ignoring facts, she refused to see a good ear specialist, preferring to mishear instructions. Deeply devoted to Edith though she was, she grew jealous and easily depressed. She disliked France, yet New York seemed no better. She made scenes, not loud ones, but scenes of grieved silence and little notes left on the table. "Oh Lord, oh Lord!" groaned Edith, already exhausted by the emotional strains of the last years with Teddy. Notwithstanding, her care for Anna never failed. When the war broke out, Anna happened to be on holiday in New York. Minnie Jones, always warmly considerate, took her in. Edith, however, would not let her sister-in-law assume her burdens. Anna could now be useful, she thought, if she were equal to helping in the work for refugees. Occupation would make her happier if she was fit for it. But was she? What did Minnie think? Could she in a roundabout way make leading inquiries about Anna's state of health? If asked directly, she would assert there was nothing wrong. In the end, Anna did return to France "as cross as a tiger" and was cared for tenderly until she died.

The case of Anna Bahlmann gives an example of Edith's concern for those who depended on her. A governess was a lady, not a servant. Anna need not appear on every occasion, but she could not be shunted off to eat in the servants' hall. No matter how trying, she was bound to be in some sort Edith's daily companion. Not money, but imagination and devotion were needed. Edith gave it all. To her dear old Grossie she was even more loving. Gross eventually became completely feeble, lost her memory, and faded into senile old age. She needed a full-time nurse. Edith provided one, saw Gross daily, rejoiced over her simple pleasures, and could not have cared more lovingly for her own mother. Mary Bagley, who had been her cook at Lenox, became another object of tender concern. When "The Mount" was sold, Edith had offered to pension Bagley, who was by then growing old. Bagley, independent, preferred a job with an elderly man, where the work presumably was easy. Edith agreed to the arrangement, but she kept in touch with Bagley, sent her a regular Christmas check, and used the occasion to inquire whether she would not now like to be pensioned. Years later, Bagley fell ill, was taken to hospital, and eventually died. Edith not only sent money for her needs, but instructed White, who was going to America, to see about a gravestone. She was horrified to hear from him that Bagley had died in a public ward, since her elderly employer had not arranged for a private room. It was a real grief to Edith to learn that an old servant had not received all the care that money could buy.

Thus, standing alone though she did, Edith was surrounded by people whose relationship, strange in modern terms, was yet most intimate. She was over fifty by now, her relatives dead or estranged, her lover unwilling to let her share his life. In her servant-family, in the company of her orange-brown little pekes and her darling old Gross, she found the uncritical love which had once been given her by Teddy. It was soothing to a temperament so restless and insecure, to a woman who had been so decisively rejected. Old age was a long way off, but she was entering upon the decline of life. The quiet simplicity of her relationship with Gross, or with Elise, her successor, would have to sustain Edith through lonely years. Strangely enough, it sufficed.

In her own immediate family there was but one real tie, that with her sister-in-law Minnie Jones. The two, always devoted, had many tastes in common. Minnie had been the first to know Henry James and had paved the way for Edith by sending him her books. It was a typical thought, for the two constantly considered each other. Minnie had her regular presents which she yearly bestowed: the *New York Social Register*, specially indexed, or an engagement calendar which Edith liked. She faithfully remembered Edith's birthday, though it came in that exhausting after-Christmas season when the best correspondent forgets. She pounced on new books which Edith in Europe might not see. She bought furs, for which Edith had a weakness. She always remembered exactly the right present for Gross or Elise. And finally she handled all the business which Edith could think of. She corrected proof when a crisis occurred, which happened often. She bought little things in New York which Edith could not get in France. Rarely can anyone of their acquaintance have left New York without carrying a consignment of Edith's special soap, her toilet water, her tea, or some other item which Minnie had got hold of. It was Minnie who sent a wreath in Edith's name if one of the numerous New York connections died, and who cabled the tidings. Minnie directed Edith's attempts to help Miss Evelyn Washburne, daughter of the rector of Calvary Church, who had fallen on hard times. In other words, Edith always called upon Minnie if anything in New York needed to be done.

In return, Edith was generous. In the twenties, for instance, she was adding a thousand dollars a year to Minnie's income, paying for a car and chauffeur for her, giving her another thousand dollars towards summer travel, and sending her a special check to celebrate the publication of each new book. She gave her extra presents, too, often expensive ones. All such occasions sent letters coming and going. Minnie was a person to whom Edith could write about her household, her daily activities, occasionally about deeper things—poor Teddy, for instance; but never, except in his last illness, about Berry. In fact, though Minnie was both relation and dear friend, some things lay too deep for discussion. In "The Fullness of Life," in the inmost recesses of the private house of her self, the woman sat alone.

No one would have thought so who had seen her in 1914, always in society and the center of a group. Edith was still branching out, enjoying new things. In 1913 she had made her first trip to Berlin. In 1914 she visited North Africa. She was planning to rent a country house in England in the late summer, revolving in her mind the possibility of spending more time there in the future. Meanwhile, that June in the suburbs of Paris the

Blanches were giving a party. It was an outdoor affair in glorious weather with tea tables under the trees and roses blooming. Inappropriately, there was some shocking news. The heir to the Austrian throne assassinated, his wife with him! Who was she? Not being of royal descent, she was kept in the background. Terrible, terrible—but far away. Edith was leaving the very next day for Spain before going to England. How should anyone be thinking of blood or war on such an occasion?

She went on her way with her friends, paying little attention. The servants had gone ahead to England to get Stocks, her place, ready, and she had time to put in. Spain drowsed in the sun, old world, off the beaten track. French papers came late or not at all.

By the end of July, a ripple of disquiet had actually reached Spain. The party got the French papers, still out of date, and thought they had better go home. They lay over at Poitiers, and all night long Edith listened to the crowds outside in the square singing the "Marseillaise." In the morning she and her friends assured one another, "It can't be war!"

But it was war in a couple of days. Edith found herself in Paris, the flat closed up and two hundred francs in her pocket. The banks were not making payments. Walter Berry, who was in Paris, gave her a little money; but he was being dunned by everybody else. Her servants in England, unknown in the small country place,

would be running short. She wired a friend over there
to lend them some cash. He wired back, "Have no
money!" She cabled her bank in New York for funds.
They replied, "Impossible!"

It was a fantastic, a nightmare situation. All the world
was upside down. Edith moved back into the empty
flat, where the furniture was carefully shrouded in dust
cloths, while she bent her ingenuity to the task of extracting money from New York. Time passed.

Eventually she got five hundred dollars at the cost of
paying a thousand; but to get it to England in any way
except on her person would be impossible. She applied
for a permit. It seemed the only thing to do; and during
this time of dislocation she felt in the way in France.
With the experience of the war of 1870 in mind, everybody was convinced that the struggle would be brief.
One mighty effort and it would be over! Meanwhile,
the daily life of France had come to a standstill.

Edith could see this for herself. Paris was a city of
very small businesses, tiny shops, little family restau-
rants. All of them wherever one went were closed,
"Pour cause de mobilisation." Papa had gone to war.
His chef, his waiters had gone to war as well. Maman
and the children could not carry on alone. Perhaps
eventually they would have to make up their minds to
do so somehow, but for the present they tightened their
belts while they waited for Papa. In an even worse position were the women from the little sweatshops of Paris,

dressmakers, makers of fine lingerie, other low-paid workers who had nothing to fall back on and were starving. Government assistance was forthcoming to some extent, but even the government was hardly organized yet. Besides, the rapid advance of the Germans threw every plan into confusion.

In this situation, Edith was appealed to by the Comtesse d'Haussonville, president of one of the branches of the French Red Cross, to organize a workroom. Surely some of the unemployed could at least make bandages! Edith, inexperienced as she was and almost totally without knowledge of the French lower class, had time on her hands. It mattered nothing that she had never so much as been inside a workroom, had no experience of charitable work save a brief, invigorating episode with the Society for the Prevention of Cruelty to Animals in New York. She was no worse off than thousands doing things for the first time in their lives. Her enormous energy tracked down an empty flat that she could use, found ladies to preside over the work in detail, collected ninety women, took a census of their abilities, and concluded that they would be much better off making hand-sewn underwear than bandages for the Red Cross like everyone else. The skilled were set to teach the unskilled, while Edith exerted herself to get orders for them, particularly from rich Americans, of whom there were a good many caught in Paris.

The work was hardly under way before her permit

to go to England arrived. Since her servants were still helpless in a strange land, she was forced to rush off. Henry James met her. Friends in England, though far less disorganized by the war, were terribly upset. They vented feelings which had been stirred up during the last weeks by the German invasion of France and Belgium.

The Great War of 1914 had been carefully planned. The German government cannot be said exactly to have desired it or to have borne all the guilt for bringing it on. But the German General Staff had long decided that a war was probable and had devoted many years to working out how they ought to wage it. One can hardly blame them for this. The French had done likewise. But the German plan unquestionably did contain features which shocked the conscience of Europe. The first of these was the invasion of Belgium, whom the Germans had sworn to protect. This was itself enough to outrage England, but some of its consequences were still worse. German hopes, like those of the French, had concentrated on a quick end to the war. Success in this depended on a rapid advance through Belgium and the whole of northern France, so as to take Paris, control the Channel ports, and make France helpless. Now it is by no means simple to overrun large civilian populations and to press on and fight important battles without taking time to consolidate one's rear. There is always the danger of sabotage interrupting one's lines of supply.

The German army, which had run into some of these troubles in 1870, was aware of the considerable dangers to their plan. Accordingly, and in the interests of a quick war, they deliberately intended to terrorize the civilian populations. Their brutalities may not seem so dreadful to a generation sated with stories of the gas ovens of Auschwitz or the tortures in Gestapo cellars of the Second World War. But 1914 should be judged not in comparison with what came after, but with what had gone before. The massacre of hostages, the sacking of villages, the burning of the great library of Louvain, the bombardment of the cathedral of Rheims, and other offenses against human life and human achievements were dreadful reminders that civilization was a veneer. To no individuals did they come as a greater shock than to such people as Edith Wharton and Henry James, both intensely civilized, both believers in that intangible thing called Western culture.

It had received a deathblow. Both perceived this, but in the confusion of that time they saw with emotion, not logic. Brutal Germany had attacked the civilized and peaceful countries on her borders. The Kaiser and German militarism were to blame. France, representing all the worthwhile efforts of the human spirit through the ages, was the victim. It is extraordinary to think of Henry James, that kindly, sedentary, civilized, aging man, talking of being seated on the stomach of William of Hohenzollern, squeezing out reparations. Edith, so much more direct and forcible than he, had little trouble in rolling up her sleeves for the fray. Her difficulty at first was that there seemed so little that a middle-aged American could do.

She went to her place in the country and made contact with her servants, but she simply could not remain there while there was fighting almost in the outskirts of Paris. At the very outset of the war, she had cabled *Scribner's Magazine,* offering an article which might have presented France to America, but she could not settle down to write it. She went to London and pestered the American and French ambassadors for leave to get back to France.

She had to wait while the Germans very nearly won the quick war for which they had sacrificed so much. Europe held its breath as the tidal wave of invasion spent itself in the battle of the Marne. Paris was saved, and the armies began to dig in. That long line of trenches which we associate with World War I began to stretch through Flanders, through northern France, and then south to Switzerland. The nightmare situation was becoming a permanent one. Edith, still haunting her embassy in London, was hurriedly given the name of a passport photographer. In those carefree days which were gone for good, there had been no passports. She hurried off, found herself in one of those London streets where all the houses are alike, and selected an entrance which bore a modest sign, "Photographer." To her surprise, she was asked to climb a ladder to the roof of a building in the backyard. Life, however, was always surprising in these wild days. Only slightly puzzled, Edith seated herself on the roof in a kitchen chair while her photographer popped his head behind a black cloth and fiddled endlessly. Presently he put out his head to apologize. "I'm so sorry, madam; but the truth is, I've always specialized in photographing wild beasts, and this is the first time I've ever done a human being." The portrait, as she says, turned out like a wildcat robbed of her young; but it got Edith back into Paris.

So nearly had Paris fallen to the Germans that the government had hastily evacuated itself and many people had fled south, including the treasurer of Edith's workroom, carrying her funds. It was necessary to find more money at once to keep things going. Meanwhile, Paris had been flooded by refugees from the north, both French and Belgian. Acquaintances of Edith's—Charles du Bos, André Gide, and others whom she had met at the Blanches'—had already organized a refugee reception center, supplementing inadequate government efforts. Edith was asked to create an American committee and to raise money. She did so with such energy and success that the care of refugees on a large and growing scale became a joint Franco-American task. It had endless ramifications. The reception committee soon needed an office and a staff of its own. A dispensary with nurses and doctors in attendance had to be established for the many who arrived sick. A clothing depot handed out garments. A restaurant provided free meals. Temporary hostels and a list of families willing to take boarders cared for immediate needs, while a committee investigated chances of employment. Family problems complicated arrangements. Many families had been separated in the confusion, and endless inquiries were necessary to reunite them. In many cases women were encumbered by small children and were untrained to support themselves while their husbands were in the army. Day nurseries were urgently needed. A workroom was set up at which women sewed one day a week for their families and the rest of the time for the clothing depot.

For such activities everything was needed: rooms, equipment, cash, and an army of workers. Edith's abilities were not of the sort which run reception centers or oversee day nurseries. She was far more useful having new ideas, discovering who had a house to lend, extracting blankets, food, medical supplies, and other contributions in kind from those who had them, dealing endlessly with the French Red Cross and other charitable organizations, which she soon discovered were in the hands of a closed clique, not so much interested in answering a need as in doing favors for influential people.

In all these ways Edith's contribution was endless. The very workrooms relied on her for materials to keep going. Meanwhile, her armies of personal friends poured in as volunteer workers. It was something, after all, to know the leisured classes of Paris. Not by any means all of the ladies who came to help were any use. Not all of them stayed. Gradually, however, the "Acceuil Franco-Américain" sorted itself out, becoming efficient through the devoted efforts of Edith herself and of a new friend, Elisina Tyler.

Elisina and her husband, Royall Tyler, had been in London before the war, where he had been editing State Papers about the diplomatic relations between England and Spain in the sixteenth century. They came at this time of emergency to Paris, where they put themselves at the disposal of Edith. In Elisina Tyler, a youngish woman in her thirties, Edith found her perfect complement. Administrative detail, which Edith did not enjoy and always threw into confusion, was Elisina's forte. Still more important, Elisina's clear mind recognized as readily as Edith's the trends of the times, the difference between permanent and temporary needs. In perfect agreement, the two women raised money, directed policy, handled committees. Between them, they made the "Acceuil" and its dependent concerns an organization which neither could have created alone.

Time swept them along from one emergency to the next. By the end of 1914, the first flood of refugees had spent itself. The mobile phase of the war was over. It had become obvious that months at least must pass before the uprooted populations could go home. The paralysis which had overtaken Paris and France in the early weeks of the war was changing to feverish activity. It became possible to settle families on farms or find breadwinners employment in Paris. There remained a residue of sick, of families whose parent was away at war or dead, of unemployables who would have to be cared for until the end of the war. Nobody imagined how far away this was, but the task of the "Acceuil" was settling down at last into a pattern.

All this was thrown into confusion by the spring campaign. The territory of Belgium had reduced itself by now to a tiny corner around Ypres and Poperinghe, crammed not only with their own inhabitants but with all who for whatever reason could not bring themselves yet to forsake the soil of Belgium. This area was to become a battleground. Ypres, under bombardment, had not only twice its normal population, but a tragic contingent of abandoned children in cellars or alleys. The curé of Ypres, exerting himself to save the children, was placing those he could collect under the care of local nuns. An appeal had been issued for the children of Ypres which Edith took up. She had already dispatched to them vanloads of food and clothing. By April, however, the situation at Ypres had become too dangerous for civilians to remain. The Belgian government was forced to arrange large-scale evacuation.

Looking around for what help it could find, the Belgian government asked the "Acceuil" to take charge of the children. The disorganization of the times confused this plan, but eventually the "Acceuil" did receive six hundred Flemish children, most of them accompanied by nuns. Once more everything had to be improvised. Large buildings in the form of country châteaux, convents, or the like had to be discovered, put in some sort of shape, furnished with bedding, supplies, kitchen and laundry equipment. Nor was it possible to set a few hundred children down in a country district and give them nothing to do. French lessons had to be organized, since they were Flemish-speaking. School books must be provided. Other activities, such as kindergartens, cooking school, community singing, training in lace-making, were devised in desperate efforts to prepare the children for life or keep them happy.

Meanwhile, other problems must be solved. Tuberculosis had been rife that winter in Ypres. Many children were infected, while among the older refugees were tragic cases. Besides the children, the "Acceuil" had been left to deal with several hundreds of the aged and infirm sent down from Belgium, also with a few attendant nuns.

For all such cases nursing care was urgent. Sanitariums for tuberculosis cannot be rough and ready. The old and ill need personal service when they cannot help themselves. The war was being fought on French soil, with the result that France was crowded with its own refugees and own emergencies, not to speak of its wounded. Edith's committee was faced with the impossible. Somehow or other the impossible was achieved, but it was done increasingly with American money. The "Acceuil," which had been started by Frenchmen, never lost its French contingent. New activities, however, belonged to its American end and took subordinate titles such as "American Hostels" or "Children of Flanders." The presiding genius and the chief money-raiser here was always Edith.

She had started looking around for money at once. She had so many connections among Americans who traveled in Europe that donations came in rapidly. Not all of them proved to be what she wanted. In the earlier and inexperienced days, she had made the mistake of appealing for blankets. Months later after she had extracted all the blankets she needed from French charitable sources, she was bitterly chagrined to get a vast consignment from America when what she needed was cash. Nor was she happier about the way in which American money poured into French charities, which she freely described as callous, incompetent, and abysses of inertia. Her own organization required three thousand dollars a month in its earliest days and twenty-five thousand at its greatest extent in 1918. Almost all of this had to be raised by her personal influence in a country she was far too busy to visit and in a period when communications with America went by ship and took their time. She wrote her letters by hand, having no secretary and being unable in wartime conditions to obtain one.

Naturally she relied a great deal on the devoted efforts of people like Minnie Jones, who personally directed most of the money-raising in New York. But business correspondence with Minnie alone took up much time, while there were also committees for raising funds in Boston, Albany, and elsewhere. Besides, contributors expected to be thanked. Poor Edith complained after going away for a short rest that she found three hundred letters on her desk when she returned.

Personal letters were not enough. Edith drafted appeals for American papers. In 1915, she took a look at the gift-books with which charities of various sorts were flooding the market, and conceived the idea of *The Book of the Homeless*. This was to be a book made up of articles, poems, stories, and original drawings by the most famous of living authors and artists of Belgium, France, Italy, England, and America. After it had come out, the original manuscripts and drawings were to be auctioned in New York. All the proceeds of both auction and book were to go to the Franco-American Hostels for the homeless children of Flanders.

It was not entirely a new idea, but Edith was in a position to collect a far more distinguished list of contributions than any rival book in the market. Theodore Roosevelt (an old New York friend) produced a foreword. Scribners promised to do the editing, protesting vainly against the use of the Merrymount Press, since Daniel Updike had his own ideas and was difficult to deal with. Edith, however, was not disposed to spare anybody effort. She herself was writing a preface with a report of the work, getting in the contributions for the book, and doing all the translations into English. She was also interfering with production details in her usual fashion. *The Book of the Homeless* became an enormously complicated work to produce. Copyright and manuscript troubles, different opinions on detail in Boston, Paris, and New York produced unending correspondence. Minnie, in charge of auction arrangements, fixed a date without notifying Updike and greatly annoyed him. After a series of crises, the book appeared. It made about five thousand dollars, while the auction netted some seven thousand more. Patient Mr. Scribner felt such modest profit was hardly worth the truly fearsome effort. Edith knew better. Business in her view always involved a great deal of trouble. Any money which could be produced for the cause was worth having. Besides, *The Book of the Homeless* had been talked about. It was advertising her needs. From all sorts of places likely and unlikely—even, she remarked with surprise, from the Wharton connection—money came in.

She was too conspicuous a person for such efforts to go unrewarded. In 1916, she was given the Legion of Honor, a decoration at that time very rarely conferred on a woman. The Belgian government later decorated both her and Elisina. Edith with a familiar tartness remarked privately that she would have preferred less

obstruction and rudeness from that source without the
honor. Even little old Gross received a medal. Edith
thought this last a great piece of nonsense; but Gross
was delighted, and she could not fail to share in Gross's
pleasure.

But Edith's activities could never be confined to the
care of refugees. She knew too many people, and opportunities arose which suited her talents. Early in 1915,
when the war was only some four or five months old,
she was asked by the French Red Cross to report on the
needs of some military hospitals near the front. This
led by an association natural to Edith's mind to plans
for making further visits to the rear of the French fighting line and publishing descriptions in *Scribner's Magazine* which would be later collected in a book.

Used as we are to the privileged position of the war
correspondent in modern warfare, it is difficult to imagine those early months of World War I. Foreign
correspondents were absolutely forbidden the fighting
areas, while even Frenchmen were limited in range and
heavily censored. Edith's descriptions made news in
America, and as she had foreseen, were valuable propa-
ganda. Trading brilliantly on the highly-placed people
she knew, she had managed to visit a number of places
close up behind the front. She had peeped through a
spy-hole in a front-line trench at a no man's land not
yet plowed up by war. She had seen the devastation in
areas from which the German armies had been driven.

She had actually watched an attack on a small scale. Indomitably, clad in prewar tight skirts descending to the ankles, she had ridden uphill on muleback and stumbled through trenches, perfectly astounding both officers and men by her appearance. No other foreigner or woman had the connections to obtain a permit from the French military, who were notoriously hidebound. Edith, invariably escorted by somebody of note, made her way everywhere, saw improvised field hospitals, picnicked in the open air, and made herself both a refreshment and a nuisance. All this, she felt, was far more her real function than the charities which now took up her time. Except for *Fighting France*, she could not write. She was too harried, and other needs were urgent. Yet never did her nature accept this situation. The long novel she had earlier started to work on was postponed, not abandoned. Organized charity was something she felt someone else could have run much better. Writing, impossible though it temporarily was, remained her job.

It turned out to be a long war. As the months of feverish activity lengthened into years, Edith's real nature had to assert itself. Yet only once in the whole four years did she write anything unconnected with the war, a companion-piece to *Ethan Frome* called *Summer*, infinitely remote in tone from the life that pressed on her. She could not find the time or strength to repeat the effort. She turned instead to writing of the war; but though she hardly knew it, the subject was beyond her as an artist. She was too much of an outsider, not exposed to the reality of the trenches, not truly French. In compensation, her ardor was too great, her tone too shrill. She still saw the war in the simple terms of 1914. It was the attack of the monstrous German military machine on culture, beauty, and the age-old spirit of France. This simplification was general enough at the time; yet suffering, sorrow, experience of horror left direct traces on far more commonplace persons. Edith Wharton, for all her fine mind, her compassion, her culture, in the last analysis lacked a personal stake.

She was burning to have one, looking forward from the very start to America's entry, never understanding how her country could hang back in such a conflict between simple good and simple bad. The years of waiting deepened her sense of being outnumbered in America by vulgar hordes whose values and standards were not hers. It might have been possible in 1914 for Edith to pick up the old pattern, regularly spending some months in her native land. It would have done her good; but by 1918, the idea was unthinkable. Emotionally, she had suffered too long with the French.

It was not that she did not welcome Americans when they at last appeared on the Western Front. She thrilled, even to the extent of writing to a mother in New York that it must be wonderful to have two sons in the war. Presently young Newbold Rhinelander, son of her favorite cousin Tom, appeared in the Air Force. Newbold was shot down and killed only a few weeks before the Armistice. Disintegration had already set in behind the German lines, and it was impossible to find out whether the boy was dead or merely a prisoner. Edith magnificently did all she could, going right to the top in her usual fashion, even putting pressure on the American negotiator of the Armistice agreement. But in her letters to her cousin Tom, genuinely helpful and sympathetic in tone, she takes lengthy occasion to regret her failure to put Newbold in touch with Paul Bourget. The boy would certainly have enjoyed the social contact with this elderly man of the world. It is a strange note to sound as consolation to a pair of grieving parents. It indicates surely that Edith is sorry, grieved, upset, concerned—and does not care. The loss of Newbold, a boy she hardly knew, does not really touch her in the inmost depths of her heart. One could not expect it, yet Edith's lack is once more emphasized. Her enthusiasm for the cause is fervent. The struggle is vital to her, and she knows it. Yet in a personal sense, she has no stake.

By 1918, Edith's health was seriously affected by overwork. She was greatly run down and her heart was giving trouble. She had taken an occasional brief rest, but her only holiday was a glorious visit in 1917 to Morocco. The French governor, General Leyautey, had arranged an exhibition to show the world the benefits of French colonial government, even in wartime. Sagely, he invited Edith as an official guest and sent her everywhere. It was a brief, delightful echo of the travels of the past; yet it was not really like those distant memories. The pace of life had become too fast. She felt it her duty to cram in all she could and to tell the world.

Even the end of the war hardly brought an end to Edith's labors. It was not possible to return Belgian exiles right away. In many cases the villages where they had lived had been shelled into fragments, trampled into the Flanders mud, covered with tangles of impenetrable barbed wire, and foully polluted by the rotting corpses of no man's land. Edith sponsored additional drives for shoes, for potatoes—anything to get people back on their feet and the country going. Many, however, were in no physical shape to be sent home. Edith's committee was running homes for old people and two sanitariums for tubercular cases, one of these a model of its kind. Such invalids must surely wait till a place was prepared, yet in the meanwhile money was harder to raise. People thought the emergency over and turned to new causes. Her best sanitarium, built with American money, was too good to dissolve. It ought to be handed over as it was to the French. Negotiations about the transfer were very complex.

Individuals are hard to fit into official categories. As the French or the Belgian government took over the problems which Edith had handled for so long, she found herself left with an increasing number of hard cases who became in effect her personal dependents. A few of those, too, who had been employed to run the workroom or in similar jobs elsewhere proved difficult to re-establish in civilian life. Edith as usual was mindful of such connections, took infinite trouble and laid out money. Her own financial situation without being desperate was disquieting. During these last years her income from her writing had naturally dropped. The value of her investments in New York had fallen also. French and American income taxes had been imposed. Prices were rising. Her vast apartment in the Rue de Varenne was more than she ought to afford. "I shall take a very small place," she wrote to Minnie, "and hang onto my motor till the end."

In fact, of course, she did nothing so drastic. It was Elisina who found her the perfect house at St. Brice-sous-Forêt, out in the country a few miles north of the Paris suburbs, not too far out to get in for the day. It was an eighteenth-century house in bad condition but with the remains of a beautiful garden, including old fruit trees and magnificent elms. She bought it immediately before the war ended. It was the spring of 1918, the moment of the last, most desperate German push which very nearly burst through the Allied lines. The Pavillon Colombe, sitting directly on the line of the German advance and under the trajectory of Big Bertha shelling Paris, was for sale fairly cheap. The tremendous alterations which Edith insisted on could only be planned. But she looked forward to her new domain as a haven of peace.

Chapter 8

FIGHT WITH A NEW WORLD

HENRY JAMES had died in 1916. He had never really recovered his health; and then besides, the war had shattered him. Aging, impractical, fitted for nothing useful, he felt for the first time the helplessness of the looker-on. To him as to Edith the war presented itself as a German attack on all he loved and valued. Yet even his writing could not serve war needs. In the course of a lifetime, he had hammered out his own style and found his subject. They did not suit the times, but he could not now change them. Anguished by his situation as a neutral, he took the step of acquiring British citizenship. The empty, futile gesture represented true bitterness of soul. War had invaded the magic world he lived in, violating the instincts of his civilized, kindly nature. Passionately desiring to resist, he could only wring his hands.

His death was a real loss to Edith. Henry James had represented her contact with greatness. He was the nonesuch in her life, head and shoulders above the rest of the world. A future without him was bound to be a meaner thing. Howard Sturgis, who represented to his friends the enduring tradition of James and the Jamesian circle, survived only a few years after the war. Edith Wharton, always a great lady in her own right, was left with nobody who could really stand up to her. A certain arrogance, inbred since her earliest years, was fortified. It became too naturally the product of her success and her armor against failure.

Success and failure were both now hers, strangely intermingled. The shattering experience of the war had made her uncertain where she stood in a world which she perceived would be different. She could not go back to the novel which she had begun four years before. It was, she realized, out-of-date. Nor could she catch her breath by contenting herself with short stories, masterpieces of mere technique. She felt charged with big ideas, and her creative powers, dammed up through the war years, were bursting forth. Her instinct, essentially a wise one, was to look backwards for a while.

The Age of Innocence, which appeared in 1920, is in many ways the best of Edith's novels. Set in the 1870's, in the time of her own childhood, it recaptures with masterly ease the flavor of the world. Its dowagers, its men-about-town, its rich descriptions are never beside the point, which really is a study of that society. Newland Archer has become engaged to May Welland. The alliance is eminently proper, and in addition he feels himself in love. May is a fresh young thing brought up conventionally and possessed of an innocence which, though artificial, is for the present charming. She has never been confronted with any serious issue, allowed to bruise herself against unpleasant facts, or educated in intelligence and taste. Newland Archer imagines that it will be sweet to enlighten her, but he soon finds her development has been stunted. She is not capable of the passion, the growth, the understanding that he requires. He falls out of love with her and into love with her cousin Ellen, brought up in Europe and separated there from a wealthy, sophisticated husband who has treated her badly. But by the same degrees that he recognizes his true passion, the family sees it too. They close in around him, driving him into May Welland's arms because he is not brutal enough to break away. Ellen returns to Europe. Newland Archer endures his prosaic marriage, brings up his children, does his duty, and does not have such a bad life. He has certainly sacrificed his personal inclinations, but the community as a whole is better off. He has been more useful as a member of the group than he could have been as a social outcast. Newland is satisfied with his choice, though many years later when the chance to renew acquaintance with Ellen comes, he lets it go by. He has grown too dull for her, and he thinks it better not to spoil the memories of youth.

The Age of Innocence is a beautiful novel, though somewhat nostalgic. Gone is the protest we sense in *The*

House of Mirth, where a trivial society destroys its devotee. Newland Archer falls very far short of being a
great man, and the society which swallows him up is
sadly limited. Yet Edith Wharton backs both. Newland
was right, she concludes, to sacrifice himself and Ellen.
The duties imposed by the standards of the time were
worth assuming, dull though they might be. *The Age of
Innocence* is, in fact, the sort of novel more fitted for the
end of a career than a beginning. Edith's powers have
not failed her. Never is her style more brilliant, are her
powers of analysis more sharp. The trouble is, one cannot precisely see in what direction she is going to develop next. *The Age of Innocence* has nothing to say to
the modern world, except that the standards of the old
were not really too bad. Masterpiece though it is, the
book represents to Edith a chance to escape a chaos of
impressions she has not yet sorted out. If so, the burning
question still remains: What will she say to the emerging
new world? She is nearly sixty, and the pattern of her
life was set long ago. She is almost a museum piece by
now with her butler, her chauffeur, her eighteenth-
century house, her gardeners and personal servants.
What aspects of modern life will she try to comprehend?
And can she do it?

The Age of Innocence restored to Edith her prewar
reputation. It won her the Pulitzer Prize and relieved her
from having to worry about hanging onto her motor to
the end. In fact, it ushered in Edith's years of greatest

earning. Its dramatic version was her first stage success and gratified her hugely by really lavish profits. It also called forth in a letter to Minnie detailed instructions about costume and appearance, ranging from the cut of mustaches, through the violets in men's buttonholes by day, the gardenias by night, and on to the question of vocabulary. Always a purist, Edith is becoming a bore on the subject of slang. It seems to crystallize every thing she does not like about America, hitting at once her sense of style, her dislike of modern standards, and her growing admiration for the past. This latter now seems an obsession. It is obvious that the dramatic version of *The Age of Innocence* was very lucky to have been presided over by Minnie, who unobtrusively gave all the proper advice, attended the opening, and sent the leading actress yellow roses from the authoress—who did not think of it until the occasion was over. If Edith in person had been taking a hand, she might have smothered the production in masses of detail.

The American public had taken another look at Edith Wharton and it still found her good. The critics, however, who in the prewar years had recognized her as a leading American writer, were beginning to hold back. The Pulitzer Prize, which is awarded not for the best novel of the year, but for that most faithfully upholding the American tradition, was won by *The Age of Innocence* in 1921. Edith, who was aware that these two things in practice were very much the same, laughed at it a little as a Virtue Prize; but she was pleased. All the greater was her chagrin when some of the facts behind the award came to light. The prize is given by the trustees of Columbia University, who as a rule are guided by the recommendation of a selection committee of experts. In this case, however, it happened that the committee had recommended Sinclair Lewis' *Main Street*. When the award was not given to Lewis, they published a letter, complaining in effect that, having been summoned to give the board advice, they did not like being disregarded. The situation was an exceedingly awkward one for both authors. Sinclair Lewis, clumsy, thin-skinned, his own worst enemy, took his revenge by declining the Pulitzer when offered him some years later. He gave as his reason a conscientious objection to the award of such public prizes, but underlined the real cause by accepting the far more valuable Nobel Prize. Edith, whose position was more humiliating than his, received an account from her New York friends of the intrigues which had produced her selection. True or false, it affected her with deep disgust. No question of merit, apparently, had entered in. It confirmed a growing aversion to the trends of American life. America's rejection of the League of Nations, the scandals of the prohibition era, short-sighted obstinacy about war debts —all the excesses of the twenties came or would come to fortify this feeling. In every contact except old personal ones, Edith found herself repelled by American life.

True, she was making money. Before the war this had
caused her to think hopefully of the growth in taste of
the American public. Now, it merely confirmed her in
her contempt for critics without raising her opinion of
her readers. Manifestly Edith was adrift. She was losing
the clarity and fearlessness of her earlier attitude. She
was thinking with her emotions.

Even in Paris she was out-of-date, and not merely in
Paris, but in the international artistic life which made
Paris its center. For America had come to Paris, not so
much to study art as to write. In fact, the war in Europe
had opened the eyes of American young men to the intellectual climate there. They had become conscious of
exactly what Edith had found, an extraordinary stimulus
which did not exist at home. Their reaction was similar.
They had to have it. The fall of the franc made it possible to scratch along in France on a pittance, or on hope
and nothing at all. They came in droves. Some blocks
on the Left Bank in the Latin Quarter soon became almost English-speaking. Americans had their own favorite bars where, over a glass of something cheap, they sat
and argued half the night about ideas. They were drift-
ers, time-wasters, no-goods, serious artists, people of
talent, and people of none. There were John Dos Passos,
Ernest Hemingway, many of the future great names in
the newspaper world, and a mass of minor writers who
underlined the tendencies of their age. All these were
in a state of revolt against the past. They hated the ma-

terial smugness of their own background, their religious traditions, their moral laws, much of which Edith had also seen and despised. With it also, they rejected her world, that wealthy aristocratic world of civilized culture which had produced, or at least had not prevented a World War. The influential schools of the times were the Surrealists, occupied with the Freudian horrors under the surface, and the Dadaists, apostles of sheer nonsense, who rejected everything and mocked at the world.

Such people did not make Edith's acquaintance. For one thing, the circles in which they moved were not the same; and for another, they despised her. Obscure and on the verge of starvation, they spurned success. When Sinclair Lewis, far more nearly their own type than Edith, appeared in Paris, they ostracized him. Lewis had committed the supreme offense: he was popular with the public. It was a reaction which Edith should logically have shared.

Pitifully enough, she was not fossilized. She was honestly making an attempt to appreciate excellence where she could find it. Sinclair Lewis, for instance, though a very different writer from herself, was in some respects the other side of the same coin. Despising the material standards of the Midwest, he wrote about them with meticulous scorn. Despising them also, she preached culture. Though Little America rejected Lewis, Edith received him and accepted with pleasure the dedication of *Babbitt*. She made a similar and very creditable effort with Scott Fitzgerald, the typical writer of the young twenties, though his rejection of all discipline and standard was antipathetic to her. Wildly flinging copies of *The Great Gatsby* around, Fitzgerald had sent one to Edith. Her answer is highly intelligent and surprisingly appreciative of his work. When he came to Paris, she invited him—to tea! He went, and she had a selected little group of literary souls to meet him in the meticulous drawing room of her perfect house. As out of place there as she would have been in a bar, he lost his head, accused her of being out-of-date, and tried to shock her. When he saw that she was not shocked, but merely curious about his experiences, he gave up and rushed out. Returning to his Zelda, he got drunk, groaning, "They beat me, they beat me!" He would have been consoled to learn of Edith's comment in the privacy of her journal: "Horrible!"

The encounter was typical. Edith had never been able to step out of herself, even for Henry James. To such writers as were possible in her drawing room, were they French or American or English, she gave real help. She always thought it worthwhile to take the trouble for beginners which Walter Berry had first done for her. She even pressed money on impecunious writers. "Take it. I have it. All that matters is that you should be free to finish the job." Such protegés, however, were far remote from the angry young men of the twenties, who were equally busy tearing down her world and their own.

In such a situation, expatriate, and with a growing distaste for modern life and especially all that America stood for, Edith had found in *The Age of Innocence* a safe refuge. She had not put a foot wrong because it did not raise the problems which concerned her in the new world. As these, however, pressed more and more heavily upon her, she faced the question of whether to tackle them or not. It was certainly arguable that by limiting herself to the prewar world, she could uphold standards which were in danger of being forgotten. By doing so, however, she would renounce her position as a leader in the American literary world. She did not want to become the grand old lady, looking backwards into her brilliant past. She did not feel old. Besides, her dislikes were getting stronger than her likes. They stared at her out of every newspaper and review. They met her on the street. Edith Wharton, who had come out of four years of war still fighting, had not the temperament of a quitter. In fact, there was never any serious question of what her choice would be. Undaunted, she sailed into the fray.

The sorry list of her failures is hardly worth too much detail. Edith had not realized, though Sinclair Lewis could have taught her, that to write of what you hate is only possible if you know it exceedingly well. It was useless to base background for a serious novel on the stories culled by Teddy at Hot Springs about life in the Midwest. It was silly to describe the bungling of a social do-gooder without considering what inner pressures drove her on. It was injudicious to select as a situation a tragedy of neglected children. This had tempted her, no doubt, because she did know the habits of the wealthy international set with their quick divorces and their spoiled selfishness. But she did not know children, hardly ever met them, and was stiff and nervous when she did. In 1913 she had represented a little boy as sobbing himself to sleep because his mother had forgotten a very dreary birthday party, consisting of his grandparents and some of their connections. It was, as we discover, his *second* birthday. She had not observed children since.

Even more distressing were Edith's lapses in taste. Her style declined first. She whose perceptions had always been so sensitive and sharp now sank to the sentimentalities of soap opera or the conventional slickness of second-rate magazines. Before the war, Edith had haughtily refused an offer from *Cosmopolitan* in spite of the money. It was beneath her, she explained, to appear in a Hearst publication. The necessities of her war charities seem to have swept aside all scruples. She was now frankly prepared to put up with the cash. Yet the deterioration of her work cannot be due to this cause. The most one can say is that easy success concealed what she was doing. *Glimpses of the Moon*, which is surely her worst novel, always sat high on her list of favorites. It seems most probable that in the rough-and-tumble of her desperate fight with the world, she was losing her head. It was the slaps she delivered which were beginning to count, not the patient undermining of a fortified position.

The truth is, Edith's subtle powers of observation were being eclipsed by a hasty irritation which had nothing to do with art. The following quotation from *The Mother's Recompense*, published in 1925, is all too typical of her later mood.

"Again the sameness of the American face encompassed her with its innocent uniformity. How many of them it seemed to take to make up a single individuality! Most of them were like the miles and miles between two railway stations. She saw . . . that one may be young and handsome and healthy and eager, and yet unable, out of such rich elements, to evolve a personality.

"Her thoughts wandered back to the shabby faces peopling her former life. She knew every seam of their shabbiness, but for the first time she seemed to see that they had been worn down by emotions and passions, however selfish, however sordid, and not merely by ice-water and dyspepsia.

" 'Since the Americans have ceased to have dyspepsia,' she reflected, 'they have lost the only thing that gave them expression.' "

When an artist's subjects actually begin to look all

alike to him, the time has come for him to paint something else.

Edith had lost her touch; but worst of all, she had lost her temper. It is almost unbelievable to discover that with her back against the wall, Edith is not a lady. Her anger about the Pulitzer Prize, for instance, was completely justified; but her revenge is not. In *Hudson River Bracketed*, Vance Weston, the hero, has written a first novel which is a success. His publishers put him forward for the *Pulsifer* Prize, which is nominally awarded by a committee, but actually by Mrs. Pulsifer, widow of the donor. Vance, introduced to the lady, finds her an aging, predatory hag who attempts to get her claws into him, discovers after various approaches that he is married, and drops him like a hot potato, transferring her affections and the prize to somebody else. Even Edith could scarcely pretend that this disgusting picture bore a real resemblance to the situation in which the Pulitzer Prize was awarded to her. And if it had, her attack in a work of fiction under so thin a disguise is appalling taste. She had put up with the award, though it had been surely in her power when the facts came out to have resigned it. Nor does she seem to have had any conscience in the matter. In 1935, Zoë Akins' dramatic version of Edith's novelette, *The Old Maid*, won the Pulitzer Prize for drama. Quite unembarrassed, Edith merely remarks that the prize should benefit the play, which was piling up royalties for her.

One hardly recognizes Edith Wharton. It seems impossible that she should have sunk to this, or that her reputation could have survived such a decline. The truth was, however, that her work in the twenties was not so much hopeless as patchy. Mingled with all the venom, the slipshod writing, the superficial knowledge, there were still passages of great beauty. Among the monkey-faces of Edith's *The Children*, for instance, one sees a middle-aged man following like a sleepwalker a mirage of youth, while a middle-aged woman who loves him watches him go. Edith's creative powers are not dead. They are merely obscured by a situation for which she is not fitted. Remembering how little guidance or help she had in these postwar years, we may at least admire her vigor. Unhappily, energy and courage are not art. The strongest convictions about the value of beautiful things will not of themselves produce great writing.

With her usual intelligence, Edith pinpoints her own trouble. Looking back over her literary career, she remarked that either it amounted to nothing at all, or else just possibly to a great deal more than anybody dreamed of. She meant that she was standing for the permanent values in European culture. The new generation was in a great hurry to tear the past down, yet perhaps the experience of ages has something to say to the future. If so, then Edith would be justified not by her achievement, but by the stand she had taken. In other words, she had come to value what she said for the sake of its message.

As the twenties wore on, critics whose opinions mattered wrote less of Edith Wharton. Her day was over. Yet the public loved her still, and the honors accorded to *The Age of Innocence* came flowing in. Chief of these was a Doctor of Letters from Yale, for which she consented to cross the Atlantic again. No honor could have been more genuinely to her mind. She, whose scholarship was entirely self-taught, had now been publicly placed on a pinnacle shared by learned men. She owed the distinction to no one. It was her achievement. The reputation of Yale was such that even in Europe where American colleges were little regarded, she wore her doctorate with pride. This seemed a moment when she might gracefully go home to New York and knit up ties which had been broken by her divorce or by long absence. Edith went. She stayed a week.

It was her last sight of her native land. She had never been home since her divorce from Teddy in 1913, and it was now too late. She fled back to Paris, pleased and proud, but yet more alien to the land where she had been brought up. Columbia asked her to come over for a doctorate some years later, but she put Columbia off. Crowds repelled her, and the iron frame which never had shown signs of exhaustion now at last was unequal to the strain. She could not face the effort, and her heart was giving trouble. Nor had she cared to see old acquaintances. People who loved her could visit her in Paris. Faithful Minnie kept her supplied with the *Social*

Register and cabled the deaths of friends. But over and over again Edith simply replied that she did not need the *Social Register* any more, while a letter would do just as well as a cable to announce the death of someone whom she had not seen in the flesh for twenty years.

She had remade her own life in France, where the work of the war years had made her feel she belonged. The speculative boom of the twenties and her increased earnings had very shortly done away with financial anxiety. Her new house, the Pavillon Colombe, at St. Brice-sous-Forêt, was in her view a small one. She called it her toy house and wrote apologetically that until she had built a little wing on the site of the orangerie, there would be no room in the servants' quarters for a guest to bring her maid. But the little wing was very soon constructed; the little garden was enlarged by moving the kitchen garden across the road. Edith had her rose garden, her orchard, her lily pool, and overshadowing trees. Indoors she had her drawing room, still tidy, her library with its tall windows, its low tables scattered with books, and its collection of flower paintings. Everywhere in the house were bowls of garden flowers.

Pavillon Colombe was a place of flowers. Into her garden Edith sallied in the late morning, her day's writing over, her letters dictated. She had a secretary at last and could cast care behind her as she put on her broad-brimmed hat, took up her garden basket and her clippers, and bustled out with her toy dogs at her heels. There were always dead roses to snip or some shrub which had managed to put out a shoot in the wrong direction. In Edith's garden, as in her drawing room, things had to behave. There were happy conferences with the head gardener over new plans, or head-shakings over some rare plant which had ungratefully not responded to special feeding. Edith still changed for lunch; she changed for tea; and of course she changed for dinner. In between such disappearances, she had her lazy hours on the terrace, talking and laughing with her endless procession of guests. She had her afternoon country drives and her visits to Paris. She had also her charities, a list of poor people left over from the war and others added at the request of friends. To these she gave time and thought as well as money. She had her annual bazaar for the curé of a parish in the industrial section in Paris. In the main, however, hers was a luxurious life and a relaxed one. When the weather began to get unpleasant, she simply departed to spend the winter on the Riviera.

The Bourgets had a place at Hyères. Edith and Teddy had gone there to get away from the worst of the winter in the years when Teddy's health had been important. Now Edith bought herself a house, a long, two-story building with a castellated turret at each end, built on a hillside with a little Romanesque church below and the dominating ruins of the ancient Château d'Hyères behind and above. This last commanded a gorgeous view of sea and mountain and rocky island. Edith with her usual passion for improvements never rested until she owned the craggy height, the ruins, and the view. She had a head gardener here, too, as well as a broad hat and gardening basket. A lovely series of terraced gardens crept up the precipitous hillside, each supported by rocky retaining walls hung over with ivy or roses. Here too there were flowers everywhere. One terrace was a sheet of freesias under two dark and shiny rows of lemon trees. Another was a mass of tulips. Tiled paths were bordered with hyacinths, alternately blue and pink. Flowering shrubs of all descriptions blazed with color.

Between these two beautiful spots, Edith's life settled down. In late October, she moved into a Paris hotel while her servants put her house away for the winter and opened the other. Here she saw her Paris friends, who otherwise came out on occasional visits. In the spring, while Sainte-Claire-le-Château at Hyères was being closed, she went on a trip. Her travels still continued, though they were getting fewer and shorter. In 1926, however, she chartered a yacht to see the Greek islands, which she had not visited since the trip Teddy had encouraged long ago. In her sixties though she now was, Edith gamely insisted on sleeping bags and mosquito netting, willing to rough it if she must, but not to miss anything. Luckily, Greek roads and transport had improved in thirty-five years, so that the party was able to sleep on board, and her endurance of anything worse than donkeyback was not tried. The Aegean was even lovelier than she remembered, and her friends were utterly congenial. Edith inclined to be demanding of other people's time and somewhat impatient if they had other ties, but she offered much.

She was seldom without visitors. All her world came to Paris. A select Christmas party grew up as a tradition of Hyères. A series of visitors were glad to escape the fogs of London, the slush of Paris, the ice of New York in order to picnic with Edith in the sun and balmy air, to race with her nimble mind through the world of literature or art, to raise tolerant eyebrows at her dogs, to hold their sides with laughter, and to refresh themselves with a taste of luxury.

They were devoted to Edith, these friends; but the group had changed. Henry James and Howard Sturgis were dead. Minnie Bourget had broken down completely; and her husband, devoting himself to her, saw nobody. Most of Edith's men friends by now were younger than she. Women she had dominated always. Now she reigned as an unchallenged queen for whom the right seat must be found, and to whom younger writers were introduced as an honor. Her secret shyness still tormented her, so that these chance encounters were by no means easier than the earlier ones when she had worn her prettiest clothes but had not dared to speak. Only now she laid down the law to cover her feelings. Somerset Maugham recalls how he was introduced to Edith, who sat enthroned in a chair and spoke to him brilliantly about French literature. Unfortunately, he had opinions of his own which she did not ask for. Cocteau he could not abide, and Gide he thought simply silly. Presently he began to feel annoyed at being lectured, and he broke into the conversation to ask her what she thought of Edgar Wallace.

Edith, cut off in full spate, drew herself up. She had not, or she wished to pretend she had not heard of Edgar Wallace.

"Don't you read thrillers?" pressed Maugham, perceiving with glee that he had drawn blood.

"No," Edith told him shortly. The truth was, she adored a good murder mystery on occasion; but she knew rudeness when she met it, too. She looked around. "It's getting late. . . ."

Needless to say, Maugham never became one of her court. He never penetrated beneath the self-assurance which her position made it easy to assume. Yet even those who loved her these days did not get far. She laughed with them as readily as ever. She was as generous of the good things which she owned, as glad of their company. But people saw her only in festive moments. If sadness or fatigue came over her, she slipped away. Many suspected an inner loneliness, but few had a glimpse of it. They only saw her eyelids flutter as she looked restlessly about her rooms for anything that might be out of place, or they noticed how her fingers were never still, busied with smoking cigarette after

cigarette or opening and shutting her gold-handled eye-
glass as she turned the pages of a book to find a reference.
They complained that her attention was too rapidly
distracted, that her conversation broke off incessantly
to deal with something that did not seem important. Few
remembered her being sad, yet few thought her happy.

One person knew her better. Walter Berry had not
remained long with the International Tribunal. Evidently the climate of Egypt did not suit him, and he had
earlier had tuberculosis. At all events, Walter Berry had
retired for reasons of health in 1911, when he was only
fifty-two. He settled in Paris, where Edith took pleasure
in sharing her intimate friends with him. People thought
of them as a pair, and an odd-looking pair they must have
appeared. Walter Berry was immensely tall and thin,
giving the impression of having been stretched at the
wrists and neck and angles to almost curious proportions.
His head was smallish and round, his hair and mustache
as thick as ever, though now turning white. His deep-set
eyes and great beak of a nose gave him a bird-like appearance, increased by the formality of morning coat,
striped trousers, stiff upstanding collar, and shiny top
hat, which were his usual costume. Age had not deprived
him of looks. It had made him impressive. Edith had not
been so lucky. Never a real beauty, she had been pass-
able with her bright brown hair elaborately done on the
top of her head and her willowy Edwardian costumes
flounced and ruffled at collar, hem, or sleeve. She had

always dressed well and still did, but she had lost her trim figure. Her bright hair had faded and was dressed in simpler modern style. It now did nothing to counteract the effect of the over-large jaw which had always made her look a trifle grim. The sacklike costumes of the twenties were particularly unkind to her matronly shape. In fact, for all her youthful quickness of movement, Edith was a dumpy, plain, and aging woman. Walter Berry, unfortunately, liked his ladies thin.

That was part of the trouble about Walter Berry. He adored flirtations. Even in his sixties, his wit, his manners, and his worldly wisdom seem to have made conquests easy. Edith Wharton was no doubt his special friend. He shared her intellectual tastes and enjoyed her company. He relied on her to make him intimate in the circles in which she moved. But prettier ladies attracted his attention too, in a different way; and he made no effort to conceal the fact. Nor did he take pains to share his life with her as she did hers with him. No friend of Edith's ever reached intimacy without knowing Berry as well. Yet Proust, who knew Berry, was not introduced to Edith Wharton.

There must have been many and many a private frustration in Edith's life resulting from her moving in the same circles as Walter Berry. She did not cease to love him with her whole heart, but she must have struggled not to expect too much. She had no rights in the matter. There was nothing to prevent him from taking what she offered and giving little. Nor could she claim sympathy if she felt jealous. Her situation was greatly eased after the war when her house in the country and her absence at Hyères for the whole of the winter reduced her casual contacts. He was still her most welcome guest. She traveled with him. She saw him in Paris when the servants were closing her house for the move and she shifted her quarters in town to a hotel. But the daily question of what he did or where he went tormented her less.

All the same, she showed what she felt. Like Edith, Walter Berry was almost alone in the world. He had a widowed sister who had kept house for him in Egypt and now lived in Paris. Apart from Natalie, however, he had no close kin. In the twenties a young cousin, Harry Crosby, appeared in Paris with a vivacious wife. The pair were both poets, extremely advanced in their views and as impulsive and irregular in their private life as their imaginations suggested to them. Walter Berry took a little of a fancy to Harry and also to Caresse, who though devoted to her husband had a lively sense of mischief. They in their turn found him impressive with his courtly manners, his truly brilliant mind, his perfect flat filled with selected treasures of Egyptian art, his mink-lined greatcoat, and the wicked little gleam in his elderly eye. Caresse consented to act as hostess for him at little luncheons—perfectly proper, she felt, since he was a cousin. She noted, however, without any trouble that Mrs. Wharton did not like her. She was well aware why.

At the end of 1926, Walter Berry had an appendec-
tomy. His sister Natalie had recently married for the
second time and gone to America. Edith, who was in
her Paris hotel while the servants closed her house, took
charge. There were no complications, and he conva-
lesced at Hyères. Returning to Paris, he took up his usual
life and even played tennis. Thereafter, he had a stroke.
It did not paralyze, but rendered him speechless and
greatly impaired his powers of reading and writing. Distracted, Edith rushed again to Paris, cabled his sister on
every possible occasion, and devoted herself to restoring
his health. Everything went wrong at once. Natalie,
though implored to remain calm, set sail for France,
alarming her brother by her prompt arrival. Walter was
irritable and nervously upset, while the doctors spoke
gloomily of a relapse unless he would be quiet. After
seeing him better, Edith posted away down to Hyères
in order to receive him there again, only to discover that
her darling dogs were ill. She imported a wonderful vet
from Cannes who pulled them round by doses of caffein
and camphorated oil and teaspoons of champagne. Her
distraction was increased by Natalie's suggestion that
Edith had panicked and alarmed her unduly. Walter was
angry. He was ill, and the sun no more shone.

It was never really to shine again for Edith. Walter
lingered all through the summer months and died in October after a final stroke. His mind was lucid till the end.
In fact, the day before, she had been talking to him of

dear old times, holding his beloved head on her arm. He could not speak to her, but he pressed her hand as he remembered.

This was all her consolation for the loss of somebody to whom her heart had been entirely given. Walter Berry was not hers even in death. He had made Harry Crosby his heir and had bequeathed to him all his personal effects, save those of his books that Edith wanted. She wanted many. Had she not looked at them with him, read them, discussed them? What else had she from the great friend of her life? The Crosbys, indifferent to her feelings, thought her grasping and did not scruple to say so. There was trouble about the burial of Walter's ashes. Natalie, too, was upset by Harry Crosby. It was all calculated to make Edith feel an outsider, though she mourned Berry as no one else could have done. What did the Crosbys care? What were Natalie's feelings, absorbed as she must be by her new married life?

Edith recovered from the blow. It was not in her nature to be prostrated entirely. Nothing, however, was quite the same or ever would be. Gallantly, she planned a trip to Syria for the spring, but was too ill to go. A year later, she was very ill indeed; and there was great question whether she would not follow Walter Berry to the grave. She recovered, thanks to a good constitution and much nursing, and with Elisina's help. It was very striking how the most intimate of all her friends had become Elisina Tyler. The two had worked together.

They were still associated to some extent in Edith's charities. In all the suffering they had seen and the work they had shared, they had grown to know each other well. It was to Elisina that Edith now turned when she needed help. Both her brothers, so long estranged, were dead. Dearest Minnie was eighty, and New York a long way off. Edith's only niece, Beatrix Farrand, daughter of Minnie and Freddy, was middle-aged, married, and absorbed in her own affairs. She had never been close. There were various people in Edith's little court who had known her longer and were nearer her own age than Elisina. But the transition from being a bounteous hostess to depending on the kindness of a guest was very great. Elisina, who had always worked with Edith, was easier to turn to.

Edith recovered, but was never quite as strong again. Her heart now gave trouble if she did not live a regular life. Ambitious travel was a thing of the past. Old age pressed upon her. New cares came with it. The crash of the stock market in 1929 and the world-wide depression affected Edith's income. She was not ruined, and it may seem hard to sympathize with the troubles of a wealthy woman with no one very close to inherit her money. But Edith was too old and too ill to make changes. She had her two houses and employed twenty-two servants, including gardeners. Many of these people had been with her so long that getting rid of them on any pretext whatsoever was not to be thought of. They looked to her for

pensions, and would receive them. Meanwhile, various
of her charitable cases were affected by the depression
and needed more help. Edith worried, not because she
need have done, but because the future was uncertain
and her hands were full and her strength was failing. She
even wrote more slowly now and had done nothing to
speak of for a whole year because of illness.

The world recovered slowly. Stock market prices began their gradual climb. Edith's earnings, in spite of her
lowered output, were not exhausted. There were movie
rights to dispose of and the dramatic version of *The Old
Maid* to bring in money. Edith's health and spirits rose.
It is even possible that relieved of the torment of Walter
Berry's presence, she gained tranquility. At all events,
old age did not seem bad. She still had her faculties,
her love of beauty, her enjoyment of good talk, good
clothes, good food. But the loneliness of life was her
great cross. Gross died. Her mind had utterly gone and
she knew no one, but it was a loss all the same. Elise,
who had taken her place and been almost as dear, died
suddenly also. Then Minnie died. She was eighty-five,
and they had been dear friends for sixty-five years. She
had represented family to Edith with her cables about
old friends, her *Social Registers*, her endless little errands, her warm letters. All this was now gone.

Friends thought Edith was turning to the Catholic
church for consolation. Walter Berry with his militantly
sceptical mind was with her no more. Gross and Elise,

devout Catholics both, had certainly impressed her with the unselfish beauty of their lives. She had always been sensitive to the beauty of Catholic ritual, of which in her long life she had seen a great deal. Her relations with the little church down the hill at Hyères were very friendly. Sainte-Claire-le-Château was built on the ruins of a convent, and there was a sanctuary to which an annual procession went right across Edith's grounds. Yet, whether or not she flirted with the notion of becoming a Catholic, she made no move. When Gross, an Alsatian, had joined the Catholic church, Edith's dry comment had been that it must be a nice change from the Lutheran faith. The remark is anti-German, but hardly that of a prospective convert. Episcopal ritual was part of Edith's background and still meant a good deal. Nor was she ever in the frame of mind required of a Catholic convert. About this time, for instance, she took up music. She knew little of it and had no gift. Music to her was a matter of intellectual effort, whereas to many it is instinctive. Yet nothing prevented Edith from forming judgments as freely and as forcibly as she had been accustomed to do in matters with which she was better acquainted. She had her opinion for what it was worth, and saw fit to express it. Certainly religion in general made some appeal to her old age. For the Catholic form of it, she probably felt old friendship and some understanding.

She was still writing, though more slowly. It was suggested that the time might have come to produce her memoirs. Edith must have hesitated. How could she, for instance, with her reticence and shyness deal with the painful subject of Teddy Wharton, who had died in 1928 after half-living for many years in his private world of illusion? What should she say of the Whartons who, she felt, blamed her for Teddy's illness and its outcome? Worse still, what could she ever say of Walter Berry? How should she treat Freddy's divorce, Harry's marriage? Perhaps it was better to handle these subjects herself than to let others do so. Many beautiful memories of old, dead friends tempted her also. In *A Backward Glance* she produced a bad book. It was hardly possible for her to do anything else, since her main object was to conceal her real self. Uncandid, however, though her memories were, they did what she required. Her private papers were going to Yale, and nobody would be allowed to read them for thirty years—after which it would not matter. For the moment, since Edith had spoken herself, nobody else would venture. She could keep her secret self free from public exposure.

Old age wore on slowly. Though never active since 1929, Edith was not an invalid. She still worked. She had taken as her last topic a raid of four American girls on English society. Rejected by the upper crust of New York, the girls are encouraged by an English governess with social experience to try the world of London. The stage is set again in the time of *The Age of Innocence*, about the period when Jennie Jerome was presented in London and Paris, when she married Lord Randolph Churchill and bore him a famous son. Edith according to custom had outlined her story, blocked it rather rapidly in, and was polishing a few climactic scenes, in between which the narrative still stretched in very slack loops. It had taken her about four years to get this far, while certainly parts of the tale had been mulled over for longer still. Edith had taken time out to write her memoirs, but she now was concentrating. It was June, 1937. She was at Hyères. Elisina Tyler received two wires on the same day. The first was from Edith announcing a heart attack and a trip to hospital, expecting, however, to return home to the Pavillon Colombe almost at once, and hoping to see her. The other was from the maid. The doctor suggested Mrs. Tyler come right away. Elisina came and was present when Edith died on August 11th at the Pavillon Colombe.

Edith had lingered about two months, conscious of what was coming and well prepared. Her will had been made, her money divided between her niece and Elisina Tyler. Her mink, her chinchilla, her jeweled "dog-collars," her Renoir painting were left to friends. Old servants and dependents had been remembered with money. It was time to be laid in the cemetery at Versailles, as close to Walter Berry as she could arrange. At her funeral it is said that the coffin, being stately and fairly massive in size to accommodate Edith, refused to go down the stairs. The gardener managed to lower it from a window, and the ceremonies duly proceeded. Poor Edith! It was not the sort of exit she would have expected.

It was not until after Edith's death that *The Buccaneers* was published unfinished. To the astonishment of the literary world, it then appeared that Edith Wharton, who had not written anything first-rate since 1920, was half-delivered of another masterpiece. Perhaps in truth *The Buccaneers* would never actually have turned out as well as it promised. But it proved that in spite of the ill-digested outpourings of the twenties, Edith Wharton had still been an authoress of powers, and that she had grown. Turning backwards once more to the world she understood, she moved with ease, treating her characters as people and not as animated signboards with a message. In such an atmosphere, her trenchant, brilliant style had come again. Against all expectation, Edith had made herself an ending for her literary life which fitted her beginnings. It was good that she should do so, for if anyone may truly be said to be dead, Edith Wharton as a person is so. Her family is extinct. The New York, even the Paris she knew are swallowed up in larger cities. Her manner of living went out before she did herself, while Western culture since the shock of the Second World War stands trembling on the edge of barbarism. Only as an author Edith lives, not by any means as one of the very first rank, yet as a distinctive one, not dead or likely to die. She makes no apologies for the many bad things she wrote. She does not need to, because her good things are a respectable collection. In the history of American literature she has her place, while in addition she is still read with actual pleasure. Not many writers can say as much. Nor would Edith seriously have aspired to more. Even in her lifetime, she gladly left the top rungs of the ladder of fame for Henry James.

Recommended Reading

BOOKS BY EDITH WHARTON

NOVELS

The House of Mirth. New York: Scribners, 1905
The Custom of the Country. New York: Scribners, 1913
The Age of Innocence. New York: Scribners, 1920

NOVELETTES

Ethan Frome. New York: Scribners, 1911
Summer. New York: Appleton, 1917
*Old New York: False Dawn (The 'Forties); The Old Maid
(The 'Fifties); The Spark (The 'Sixties); New Year's Day
(The 'Seventies)*. New York: Appleton, 1924

SHORT STORIES

Any of Edith's many collections contains some good tales. The
best single collection published in her lifetime is: *Xingu and
Other Stories*, New York: Scribners, 1916

A still better collection may be found in: *The Best Short Stories
of Edith Wharton*. Edited by Wayne Andrews. New York:
Scribners, 1958

SOME MODERN EDITIONS

Clothbound

A Backward Glance. Scribners, 1964
Summer. Scribners, 1964
Old New York. Scribners, 1964

Paperbound

Ethan Frome. Scribner Library
The House of Mirth. Scribner Library
The Custom of the Country. Scribner Library
The Age of Innocence. New American Library (Signet)

INDEX